Lucky Medicine

WELL HOUSE
BOOKS

Lucky Medicine

A MEMOIR OF SUCCESS BEYOND SEGREGATION

Lester W. Thompson

INDIANA UNIVERSITY PRESS

This book is a publication of

Indiana University Press
Office of Scholarly Publishing
Herman B Wells Library 350
1320 East 10th Street
Bloomington, Indiana 47405 USA

iupress.org

Manufactured in the United States of America

First printing 2023

Cataloging information is available from the Library of Congress.

ISBN 978-0-253-06525-4 (hardcover)
ISBN 978-0-253-06526-1 (paperback)
ISBN 978-0-253-06527-8 (e-book)

To my grandchildren: Briana, Scarlett, Noah, Luca, and Lilah

CONTENTS

PREFACE

SINCE 1619, WHEN THE first ship bringing enslaved Africans arrived in what would become the United States, slavery and its vestiges created a caste system into which their descendants were assigned. The caste determined where you could live, with whom you associated, and what jobs were open to you. In 1943, the year I was born, Jim Crow racism was systemic and firmly entrenched. Obtaining a college degree was deemed one pathway out.

In the first years of the 1960s, I was part of a small group of African American students enrolled at the main campus of Indiana University. Much has been written about the social unrest and activism that arose in the latter half of the decade, but very little has focused on its first half, particularly as it relates to the racial situation at IU. We students of color numbered no more than four hundred of the sixteen thousand or so on the Bloomington main campus at the time. In contrast to most of our home environments, the burden of racism was much less prominent at the university. For us, the first half of the 1960s marked a transition period between the world of Jim Crow from which we came and the turbulence of the second half of the decade, which we would later experience. Greek life was an integral and nuclear component of our social fabric. As I have grown older and view those years through the lens of time, I believe our set of circumstances was, if not unique, unusual and worth recounting in a book. I kept a journal during my undergraduate years so I could recall how I lived them. Though I started writing the memoir six years ago, the energy of the Black Lives Matter movement and the uprisings for social justice triggered after the murder of George Floyd added fervor to my plan to produce a narrative of that time period.

The memoir is also an American coming of age story. Integral to it is the impact two dominant men had on my life. The story highlights the role racism played while I was growing up in segregated Indianapolis, from elementary through high school. It then proceeds to illustrate some of the challenges our small group experienced at the large, almost entirely White university situated in the heart of southern (both culturally as well as geographically) Indiana. The significance of "Lucky" in the title becomes clear as the story unfolds.

The urgency to complete the book is, in part, a function of my age; I am now seventy-nine years old. I want to finish it before my time runs out. I've tapped many sources along the way to fill in the gaps in my recollections, including relatives, lifelong friends, and former IU classmates. My editors have guided me in streamlining the text and maintaining its flow and focus. To them and Indiana University Press I am profoundly grateful.

Lucky Medicine

Before

ONE

L.L. GOODMAN

THE DRIVEWAY UP TO Mr. Goodman's home on North Kessler Boulevard was narrow and winding, with a rock wall on each side leaving barely enough room for one car to maneuver. Abundant trees and shrubs partially obscured the house until you reached the top. In front, a circular driveway surrounded a large reflecting pool. In back, there was an even larger swimming pool. The house was old but impressive in style and expansive enough to have a gabled and columned entrance at either end. Time had transformed its once-alabaster walls to a dusky cream and dulled the luster of its red tile roof.

My memory of our visits date to early childhood, when everything seemed oversized. We always entered through the large front door, which may not sound significant, but this was the 1950s. L.L. Goodman was a wealthy Jewish businessman and philanthropist; my father was his Black barber. I recall the awkwardness I felt almost every time we walked in. "Hello, Cal!" was Mr. Goodman's typical greeting as he extended his hand to my father after opening the large front door. "Hello, L.L." was my father's usual response. When Mr. Goodman noticed me, his countenance would soften with a smile as he said, "Why, hello, Lester." Mr. Goodman and my father had been born in the same decade and were similar in stature. Both were about five feet, nine inches tall, balding, with glasses and a little paunch. Mr. Goodman stood ramrod straight, a posture that exuded self-confidence. His manner was direct. There was no warmth or fuzziness to his character. When he spoke, his tone was reserved and matter of fact but not uncaring. Most often he wore a collared shirt, sometimes under a sport coat with slacks. By contrast, my dad's posture was slightly stooped. No matter the season or time of day, he always wore a suit and tie. The two had known each other for more than twenty years before I was born. Over that time they had become friends, yet I observed their relationship was not one of equals. In subtle ways, my dad was always slightly deferential. His usual take-charge demeanor was muted.

Once inside, we would walk through the foyer, proceed down a couple of steps and enter the large sunken living room. The atmosphere was one of traditional elegance. I recall scanning the room and thinking, "This is really cool!" After a few minutes, I would follow the two men into Mr. Goodman's study. On the floor of the wood-paneled room was a life-size tiger-skin rug, its mouth wide open as though it was about to roar. Often I found myself thinking, "I wish we had one of those, too."

"Mr. Goodman, may I touch it?" I asked. He would nod, and I would gently move my hand back and forth over its soft fur. I don't recall giving much thought to what had happened to the tiger to get it there. Once Mr. Goodman settled into his leather desk chair, my dad would stand behind him, place the barber's drape over his chest and shoulders, secure the top edge around his neck, and proceed to cut his hair. Staring at me from two of the walls were the stuffed heads of additional hunting trophies.

Though struck by the grandeur of his home, I never felt comfortable in it. Infused with an aura of old-school wealth, it seemed stiff to me, a bit like Mr. Goodman's personality. Clearly his life was far different from ours. His home was in an exclusive White neighborhood. By contrast, we lived in a five-room third-floor walk-up apartment located not far from the city center in what was labeled Indianapolis's Near North Side. Though we never thought of it as a ghetto, all its residents were Black. This was the complexion of my world. I knew I was only a visitor at Mr. Goodman's, though my dad seemed quite comfortable there. I didn't know why my father periodically brought me along on those visits. It wasn't until years later that I learned how greatly Mr. Goodman would shape my entire future.

To augment income from his shop, which was located in a downtown office building, my father also had a chair in the men's locker room of the Broadmoor Country Club, the only Jewish club in Indianapolis. Mr. Goodman was a prominent member, and I suspect he had a hand in having the shop placed there. Most Sundays my father provided haircuts for the members before or after they hit the links. Some Sundays, when my mother would let me skip Sunday school, my dad would take me along to the club. I remember many occasions when I played outside with the Jewish kids, but one memory stands out: The club had a big outdoor pool. I was six or seven years old. It was a hot, sticky, midwestern summer day. "Come on in the pool with us!" a couple of the members' kids beckoned to me. My father made it clear that I was never to go into the pool. He didn't tell me why, though soon I figured it out.

"I can't," I replied.

"Why not?"

"I don't know how to swim."

Although this was true, I didn't admit to the other kids I wasn't allowed to swim because of my race.

My friends' parents and my own were part of the generation that had lived through the Great Depression and World War II. Since both of my parents were from the South, their world had always been racially segregated. They were forced to learn the rules of how to "get along," and they taught them to us along with the consequences of breaking them. I clearly remember Emmett Till's murder and *Jet* magazine's photo of his battered face in the open casket. Seeing no way to openly challenge the Jim Crow system, my parents grudgingly acquiesced to it. So, for our generation, this was the frame of reference. It was our normal.

The Black community in Indianapolis, my hometown, was stratified by skin color, occupation, neighborhood, which church you attended, and what social clubs you belonged to. To be a "professional" in our community was often defined by the cliché "preacher, teacher, doctor, lawyer," but barbers, like Pullman porters and waiters, were also considered professionals. In Black communities, traditionally the church played a prominent role, both socially as well as spiritually. Another legacy of Jim Crow segregation was reflected in the city's church congregations; they were essentially either all Black or all White.

Most of our family friends were either Baptist or Methodist, and there was a social hierarchy to the churches as well. Which one you attended mattered. We belonged to Bethel AME (African Methodist Episcopal) Church. There were a number of physicians, dentists, and lawyers among our congregation.

Our pastor had a PhD. I had the impression that some of our fellow Black Methodists considered themselves to be a rung or two higher than the Black Baptists, who they believed to be more plebeian. My mother encouraged regular Sunday school attendance during elementary and junior high school, and once I outgrew Sunday school, she and I often attended church services together. My father professed to be an atheist; so far as I can recall, he never set foot inside the church. Although I never considered myself to be an ardent Christian, Bethel AME Church was important to me not just socially but spiritually. I worshiped there as long as I lived in Indianapolis.

TWO

(DIS) INTEGRATION

IN 1948, THE YEAR I began going to school, the Indianapolis public schools were still segregated, so I was required to attend a kindergarten designated for Blacks, located some distance from home. Every day a man drove us there and back in a big black Dodge sedan. To us little kids, its interior seemed cavernous. It even had rumble seats in the back! Much later, I would learn we used this unregistered or "bootleg cab" because there were no school buses available to us. Our driver would pick me and two other kids up each morning and bring us back home after school.

The closest elementary and junior high school, School 32, sat only two blocks from our apartment building. While I was commuting to kindergarten, Fay, the daughter of a close family friend, was required to attend a segregated elementary school some distance from her home even though, like me, she lived within walking distance from School 32. One day when my mother and I were in the kitchen I asked her, "How come Fay doesn't go to School 32?" Apparently surprised by my question, she stopped washing dishes and paused. Then, softly, with a sigh, she replied, "She can't."

Persisting, I asked, "Why?"

"Because she's colored."

That is my first memory of race as an issue. Official segregation in the schools ended before I entered first grade the next year. Now school was sufficiently close that I could walk there. Nonetheless, de facto segregation in Indianapolis persisted. We learned which parts of the city were welcoming and which were not.

With the exception of my first-grade teacher's name, Mrs. Woods, I recall little about school at that time. Considering the determined resistance that occurred in the South after the US Supreme Court outlawed school segregation, one might have expected similar opposition in Indianapolis since its population was filled with Whites with southern roots. Although there was some resistance from the White community, I don't recall any of it directly affecting me or my friends. But very little else changed. The neighborhoods remained segregated. In my first-grade class at School 32, the racial split was close to fifty-fifty because the school district included a portion of an adjacent White neighborhood. Over the ensuing years, White flight changed the racial character of the district. My junior high class was close to 80 percent Black.

Only fragmentary recollections of my time in the primary grades persist. Once I began elementary school, the trips to Mr. Goodman's home were less frequent, but two or three times a year my dad would bring me along with him. As I grew older, I became aware that Mr. Goodman took a greater interest in me and what I was doing. I thought he was simply being polite. My dad had yet to explain why he brought me along on those visits.

One day when I was eight or nine, a buddy and I were talking about first names. Each of us wondered what we would have been called had we been born girls. He didn't know. At School 32, I realized my first name was unusual. I didn't know any other Lesters. One weekend afternoon I asked my dad, "What would you have named me if I was a girl?"

"Hattie Kay." My fraternal grandmother's first name was Harriet, but she went by Hattie.

"Why did you name me Lester?"

"You were named for Lazure Goodman. His middle name is Lester. He is your godfather."

"Oh," I thought. "That's why he brings me along on those visits. It must be to show me off as Mr. Goodman's namesake."

My middle name, Walker, was from another of my dad's longtime friends, so I concluded that was all there was to it. It didn't occur to me to wonder about the significance of being named for a rich Jewish businessman until much later.

Sometime during the first few weeks of my third-grade year, I brought a letter home for my parents. A short time later, we had a meeting with my teacher. I don't remember the specifics, but the result was she suggested advancing me early to the second semester, moving from grade 3B to 3A. My parents agreed, so I skipped the remainder of the first semester of third grade. It wasn't until I entered junior high school that I began to understand the significance of being advanced one semester.

I was a pretty good student. All through grade school and junior high I was at or close to the top of my class. Despite my academic success, the fact that I was really skinny, stammered a lot, and started wearing braces in the seventh grade challenged my self-confidence. Being advanced one semester, which put me with the older kids, only fueled my sense of insecurity. I didn't disclose my feelings to anyone, but my parents must have sensed something was amiss. After an anxiety attack caused me to miss my junior high school graduation, my dad took me to see Dr. Norris, our family physician. It was too long ago to accurately recall details of the visit, but I remember him briefly talking with me and then writing a prescription. I took the medication for a couple of weeks. Either because the medication was effective in reducing my anxiety or because of the adverse reaction of drowsiness, I discontinued it. There was no follow-up with Dr. Norris. Years later, I found the box with a few remaining pills. It was a sedative: phenobarbital.

My imperfections notwithstanding, my experiences at School 32 were generally positive. I was teased because I was tall and skinny, but I was never really bullied. At age nine I began playing the violin, and I progressed to first chair by the time I left for high school. Score a point in enhancing my self-esteem. And there was another bonus: When I reached junior high, I was offered a job of sorts. Once or twice a week, one of the primary grade teachers would show her class a movie or a filmstrip. The projectors were kept on a rolling cart in a storage room. I was offered the job of setting up the projector in whichever classroom it was needed. This was an honor because it meant I was a superior student who could leave my class a few minutes before the end of the period, retrieve the projector, set it up in the room, and then return it at the end of the class. Of course, I quickly accepted the offer. Our school was an old two-story building with no elevator. Because the projector weighed about thirty pounds, sometimes I had difficulty lifting it off and back onto the cart to carry it up or down the staircase. The teacher who recruited me must have noticed my struggle, so he assigned a classmate to assist me with the heavy lifting. Clarence was pretty buff for a junior high schooler and, like me, was more than happy to get out of class early.

THREE

MY SON IS GOING TO BE A DOCTOR

BECOMING A DOCTOR WAS a goal my father had and then set for me. He had been born in 1898 into a poor Black family in Nashville, Tennessee. I learned my paternal grandfather was thirty years older than my grandmother, meaning he was born around 1847. With a birthdate in the late 1840s, he was likely born into slavery. He died in 1907 at age sixty, when my father would have been eight or nine years old. As the oldest boy, my dad did whatever he could to help his mother and his four siblings survive, but what he wanted was to become a doctor.

I never learned what stimulated my father's interest in medicine; he never explained his reasons. I suspect one of his motivations was to receive the prestige and recognition becoming a physician would bring. He always strove to emulate the lifestyle of his wealthy customers, though it was never within his reach. He used to joke about the first European surgeons evolving from barber surgeons of the Middle Ages. But by the time he had reached his teens, since his formal education ended in the primary grades, he must have realized becoming a doctor was not attainable. Apparently, that made him determined that if he had a son, that boy would accomplish his dream for him. Had I been a girl, who knows what he would have done.

I don't recall my dad ever telling me I should become a doctor, though he frequently told just about everyone else. My father's approach to parenting was not unkind or abusive, but it was autocratic. His habit was to lay out the agenda, make sure I understood what was required, then instruct me to follow through. The items on the agenda were not up for debate. My earliest memory of wanting to become a doctor dates to age four and is enmeshed in my father telling his colleagues that was what I was going to be.

Holding my mother's hand on walks down Capitol Avenue on a warm Sunday afternoon is one of my favorite early childhood memories. Our destination was five blocks away: Methodist Hospital on Sixteenth Street. I never thought to question why it was our destination. We never entered the building. Perhaps she simply found it a convenient distance to walk with a little boy. As we approached, even from a distance we could see atop its main building the tower resembling a lighthouse with a rotating beacon in the form of a lighted cross. Those walks had special meaning. Something about the hospital garnered my attention. To me, the structure seemed massive and mysterious, but I can't explain why I was attracted to it.

Our first family physician had an office located across the street from the hospital. Only bits and pieces of my well-child visits to Dr. Levi are retained in my memory, but I clearly remember I didn't like him. He was a short, squatty man with an abrasive demeanor and no bedside manner. Every time I learned I had doctor's appointment, I feared I would have to get a shot. My mother told me that a block or so before we arrived at Dr. Levi's office, I would realize where we were headed and start to whimper like a puppy. Curiously, though I never liked the man, I recall being stimulated by something about him despite my fright. Possibly I was struck by the certainty of his manner or drawn by the mystery of the tools and instruments he wielded. Maybe it was his status as an authority figure. I can't put my finger on what it was.

One could naturally ask, "What were your dreams? What did you want to do when you grew up?" It is only now that I realize how successfully my father wrapped me inside his unfulfilled dream to the exclusion of all others. By the time I reached high school, my feet were firmly on the path to becoming a physician. Until I was preparing to submit my application to medical school, I don't remember seriously considering why I hadn't become attracted to anything else.

FOUR

FAMILY CRISES CHANGE THE PARADIGM

DURING SUMMER VACATION BETWEEN first and second grade, my dad's business failed. He leased a shop on the sixth floor of the Illinois Building, one of the major downtown office buildings. Most of its tenants—my father's customers—were businessmen, attorneys, physicians, and dentists. Besides my father, there were three other barbers, a manicurist, and a guy who shined shoes. In rapid succession all three of the other barbers left the shop. Mr. Baxter died, Mr. Madison retired, and my dad had conflicts with George (I don't remember his last name), so he also left. My father couldn't find barbers to replace them. I don't know if Mr. Goodman played any role in trying to tide him along, but in the end he had to close the shop. Shortly afterward, our family car was repossessed. At that point, my mother was a housewife, but my father's sudden unemployment mandated that she quickly secure a job to enable us to survive—especially because my father was a closet alcoholic. Possibly his drinking contributed to his business setback.

Shortly after my mother started working, my father decided to stop drinking cold turkey. It might have been that he simply could no longer afford to buy alcohol. Whatever the reason, he developed acute withdrawal, or delirium tremens, right there in our apartment. It happened on a day when my mother was working, and I was home with him. My father began hallucinating, crying out to people who weren't there and picking spiders out of the air. I didn't know what was wrong. During what must have been an attempt on his part to get out of bed, I heard a thud and a cry for help. He had caught his left foot in the fluke of the bedpost at the foot of his bed, causing him to fall. When I rushed into the bedroom, his upper body was twisted and lying on the floor while his foot was still caught on the bedpost. To free him would require lifting his leg high enough to get it over the spire atop the bedpost. I didn't have the strength to do this. Frightened, totally overwhelmed, and unable to help him, I cried, "I can't get your leg out!" I ran across the hall to get Mr. Gray, who came over, freed him, then helped him to the bathroom and back into bed. I don't remember much about the next few weeks, but I know my dad recovered.

My father had a big ego and basked in hearing his customers tell him what a great guy he was. He didn't receive that kind of praise at home, though years later I learned he desperately wanted it. While he was out of work, the role of family breadwinner fell to my mother. Before my father had lost the shop, there were frequent arguments, most often about money. After he had lost the shop, the arguments grew more intense. I never saw any sign of physical abuse, but there were psychological wounds. After a few difficult months, my father landed a job in another shop located in a different downtown office building. As best as I can remember, he remained sober for many more years, until once again his business began to fail.

My mother continued to work, partly because my dad constantly spent more than he earned. Years later, she told me how she had been able to start working so quickly. My mother had grown up in Pleasant Ridge, Kentucky, a town that was little more than a collection of farms with a post office and a general store. My maternal grandparents were tobacco farmers. Given my mother's gender and ethnicity, and having only a high school education and work experience only as a nanny to a wealthy Jewish family in a different city, she had few employment opportunities. Clearly understanding that, she appealed to Lyman Ayres—president of one of the major downtown department stores, who was also one of my father's longtime customers and friends—to find a job for her in the store. Fortunately, he provided a position as an elevator operator for her. Self-service elevators were not installed until the 1960s. Notably, the elevator operators were all Black women. Despite what could be considered a menial job, they were a proud group, standing tall in their natty uniforms. There were no Black salespersons at the time.

Being an only child led me to develop a degree of self-sufficiency. My parents allowed me greater freedom than would be advised today. The world was safer then. Fortunately, our apartment building was not only close to my school but located on a bus line that led directly downtown. In the second grade, once both my parents were working, I became a latchkey kid. It was common for grade-schoolers to walk to and from school and not unusual for them to take a bus downtown and back on their own. The neighbors on our floor usually checked on me after school. Mr. and Mrs. Gray, a kind elderly couple, lived in the apartment directly across the hallway from ours. Mr. Gray was the one who had freed my dad when I called for his help. They often served as surrogate grandparents. It seemed they were always at home and available if I needed something. One apartment down the hall from theirs lived Esther and William "Stunts" Gooch. They had no children. Stunts worked during the day. At home he was quiet and reserved; I rarely saw him. However, Esther was exactly the opposite. She did not work outside the home. Probably in her late thirties or early forties, she was upbeat, cheerful, and vivacious. Her enormous smile would light up any room. I saw her almost every day. Not only was she a very attractive woman but—I'm now almost embarrassed to note—she had a very large bosom! When she approached, even to a grade-school boy, it was impossible not to notice it. To me, Esther functioned in a space between a big sister and an aunt. She provided comfort and support when I needed it and my folks weren't available, but she maintained enough little girl energy to enjoy having fun. These folks often became my security blanket when my self-confidence floundered. It wasn't until I reached adulthood that I began to understand how much their presence and foster parenting contributed to my security and well-being.

While my father acted as the captain of the family ship, he didn't spend a lot of time at home. At day's end, after closing his downtown shop, he would often make "house calls" (he loved to use medical terminology) to the homes of some of his wealthy customers, as he did with Mr. Goodman, to cut their hair when they were unable to go downtown. My father was a talented political operative, though he didn't seek the limelight for himself. He often described his role as a "behind-the-scenes man." He was skilled at networking and facilitating connections between individuals who would be unlikely associates, because many of them were his customers. He was a valued confidant who could keep a secret. All this meant he often arrived home late in the evening. My mother would have his dinner prepared. After eating, he would retire to the bedroom. It was my mother who held the family together. Though my father provided most of the money, she managed the household finances and often had to pinch a penny until Lincoln jumped off! My discipline also fell to her. Nevertheless, she was far more compassionate than my dad. I'm tempted to use a biblical analogy: he laid down the law while she added spirit to it.

Looking back, I can't decide if we would have been considered poor. I know I didn't think of us that way. Finances were always tight, especially while my father was not working, but we usually had sufficient money to pay our bills, and we had enough food to eat and clothes to wear. But rarely were there funds for luxuries. Our discretionary income was severely limited. Major purchases were always made "on time," using layaway. We never took vacations; the trips we did take were just to visit relatives. None of our extended family lived closer than one hundred miles away. Until I finished medical school, I had never been farther than three hundred miles from home.

FIVE

MY PERSONAL GOAL

THOUGH MY FATHER MADE his plan for me to go to medical school abundantly clear, when I reached high school I had my own goals. Primary among them was to earn a varsity letter in basketball.

When one thinks of a sport in the state of Indiana, it's basketball. In the 1950s and 1960s, high school basketball was the game. Along with my friends, I played pickup games from the time we were old enough to get the ball high enough to reach the hoop. We played year-round. In the summer it was shirts versus skins. In the winter we swept the snow from the court and played in our coats until we were warm enough to ditch them. Being skilled players was our common goal. In junior high, I was the second-string center on our basketball team. Though our center was not any more talented than me, he was always the starter. I spent a lot of time riding the bench; nonetheless, I felt I was a decent ball player. Neither of my parents made it to any of my games because the games were scheduled in the afternoon, and my parents were too busy working.

I had high hopes, so when tryouts for freshman basketball were announced, I thought I could make the team. At the end of a week of afterschool practices, it was time for the first cut. The results—what was called a "cut list"—were posted on a bulletin board outside the gym. It usually read, "These boys may return to practice." Early on the day the list was posted, one of the other guys who was also trying out told me with a bit of a smirk, "We saw all of our names, but we didn't see yours." I figured he was kidding me. He wasn't. I was cut. It was my first big failure. It was all I could do to hold back my tears.

Now, I wish being cut had led me to practice harder, improve my skills, then try out for the JV team the next year, but it didn't. My spirit was broken. The reason I failed to make the team was obvious, but it took many years before I could finally admit it to myself: I was simply not good enough. I wish I could say I turned my focus toward excellent academic achievement, but that wasn't the case either. Oh, generally I tried to do my best in all my subjects, but I did not become a study nerd. Still, I finished Shortridge in the top quarter of my class. At that time in Indiana, all that was required to enroll in a state-supported school such as Indiana University was to successfully complete high school.

SIX

THE END OF THE DREAM?

IN 1956, WHEN I was thirteen and in the eighth grade, our family received some disturbing news. It was evening when the phone rang. I was closest to it, so I picked up the receiver. It was my dad. His voice was filled with anxiety. "L.L. Goodman is in the hospital. He had a heart attack today!" A flood of fear rushed over me as I passed the information to my mother. I knew almost nothing about heart disease, but I knew people who had heart attacks often died. She took the phone and asked, her voice filled with concern, "How is he?"

"They say he is stable" was my father's answer.

My fear was not only because of Mr. Goodman's health crisis. I had become aware of how much his presence in our lives meant to my father and, by extension, to my mother and me. What would happen if he died?

When my mom gave birth to me and L.L. found out that she'd delivered a boy, he had made my dad an offer. If I was given L.L.'s name, he would send me to college. For many years, I did not know what prompted this pledge. One might expect that when I was old enough to understand it, I would have been overwhelmed and jumped for joy, but that was not the case. I had no idea what going to college entailed, much less what it might cost or how my family would be able to afford it. It was similar to being told as a twelve-year-old that you'd inherit a substantial trust fund when you reached twenty-one. I probably thought, "That's nice" and continued on. It was not until midway through high school that the magnanimity of L.L.'s offer hit me, coupled with my total inability to understand why he would do such a thing! Yet even then I could not foresee the enormous impact he would have on the course of my life.

On the night L.L. had a heart attack, I witnessed my father's distress over the potential loss of his mentor and friend. When he arrived home, he was visibly shaken. Fortunately, Mr. Goodman survived; a few days after he was admitted we visited him in Methodist Hospital. This was the first time I'd set foot inside any hospital. When we arrived, not knowing what to expect, I was a bit apprehensive. The hospital had specified visiting hours, and there were quite a few others in the lobby when we arrived. A woman at the information desk directed us to Mr. Goodman's room. I remember seeing him lying in bed in his hospital gown. I didn't know what someone who had just suffered a heart attack was supposed to look like. He appeared normal to me except for the gown. "Hello," he replied as we greeted him. His demeanor seemed unchanged from when I'd last seen him.

Unknown to me, after L.L. recovered from the heart attack, he divorced his first wife, Esther, left the house on Kessler Boulevard, and remarried. Mildred, his new wife, had been his secretary. She was not Jewish. One likely reason for the split was Esther's mental illness. Her behavior was seriously bizarre. All I recall are her outlandish comments, which often bore no relationship to what was being discussed or to reality. I thought she was simply weird. I believe my dad referred to her as "crazy." I could empathize with Mr. Goodman's decision to finally give up tolerating her. I had not met the new Mrs. Goodman and didn't know what to think. In our community, divorce was frowned upon, often discussed only in hushed tones. But by listening to my father's conversations, from the visits to see Mr. Goodman, and from the time I spent with the Jewish kids on Sundays at the Broadmoor Country Club, I learned something about the Jewish community. My general impression was that marrying someone outside the faith was at best disapproved of and at worst strongly opposed. I wondered how well the new Mrs. Goodman would be received, because she was not Jewish. As it turned out, it didn't cause much of a stir at all.

SEVEN

MOVING ON UP, SORT OF

THREE WEEKS BEFORE I finished junior high, in January of 1957, we moved from the apartment at the corner of Twenty-First Street and Senate Avenue to a more upscale residential neighborhood made up of single-family homes and duplexes. My parents bought a two-story duplex, planning to take on a tenant whose rent would help pay the mortgage. Coincident with the emergence of suburbia and the end of official segregation, the White community began moving farther away from the city center, generally north. Members of the Black community followed their migration and moved into the areas the White people had vacated. Our new neighborhood was adjacent to the last upper-class White enclave south of Thirty-Eighth Street, a onetime de facto racial boundary—a gated community interestingly called Golden Hill. Our house, located in what the city designated as the Golden Hill Annex, was only two blocks away from Golden Hill's front entrance. If you think the proximity of the two communities would provide opportunities for social interaction, it didn't. We might as well have lived two miles rather than just two blocks apart.

My new neighborhood was so quiet compared to our old one that I initially had trouble falling asleep. Our apartment had only one bedroom with twin beds that my father and I occupied. My mother slept on a sleeper sofa in the dining/family room. I don't remember my parents ever sleeping together. The only space set aside for me was a desk at the end of the hallway next to the bathroom where I did my homework. In our new home, my mother and I took the two upstairs bedrooms while my father established a space for himself, using the same sleeper sofa, in the basement. Having my own room was a pleasure. Now I no longer had to share a closet for my stuff. The underlying implications of my parents' sleeping arrangement did not register with me until years later.

EIGHT

SCHOOLED

WHEN I REACHED HIGH school, it was not only a step up but a step down as well. School 32 had fewer than three hundred students; Shortridge had over two thousand. The pond had grown significantly larger, but this fish hadn't. I didn't have my father's social skills; he moved seamlessly from one group to another. Unlike in elementary and junior high school, where I had become a known quantity, I arrived at Shortridge High School in January 1957 as one of twelve incoming freshmen and the only one from School 32. Wearing braces with headgear, I did not take the school by storm. I wouldn't turn fourteen until June.

Shortridge is a distinguished high school. Founded in 1864, it is the oldest public high school in the state. Some of its famous alumni include the great granddaughter of Eli Lilly, founder of the pharmaceutical company that bears his name, who was a member of the class ahead of mine; the author Kurt Vonnegut; and former Indianapolis mayor and US senator Richard Lugar. It was considered one of the city's top high schools. Shortridge's student body came to reflect the ethnic migration in the district. During my four years there, it went through a rapid and dramatic demographic transition from what had been historically an almost entirely upper- and upper-middle-class White and Jewish student body to over 40 percent Black when I finished. At that time, Indianapolis was not an ethnically diverse city; there were few if any Asians or Latinx. Its population consisted essentially of Blacks and Whites.

Being a high school freshman is often fraught with challenges, but even now I think the ones I encountered were a bit more daunting than some others experienced. Entering at the beginning of the second semester of the school year because of being advanced early to the second semester in grade three meant I was either a semester ahead of the class in which I would have normally been a member or a semester behind the class a year ahead of mine. The question facing me was which group I would fit into more easily. Of course, I chose to try to hang out with the older kids, but I didn't realize how much the age differential would affect my social integration. It didn't take very long to find out. I was always a half step behind the other students. There was a group of individuals I'll call the "in group," which I hoped to be part of. Its members lived in the same neighborhood, had gone to the same elementary and junior high schools, and had entered Shortridge together the previous fall. I knew only one of its members, Dixie Waugh, who, like me, was one of the twelve entering freshmen that January. Like my dad, her father managed a barber shop in one of the downtown office buildings. Mr. Waugh was the person who had hired my dad after his shop had failed. Dixie didn't live near us, was three months older, and had attended different elementary and junior high schools. We were not yet close friends. Nevertheless, she was a member of the in group, and knowing her would serve as a segue into it.

The person who really facilitated my entry into the in group was one of Dixie's longtime friends, Steve Talley. How I came to know Steve is lost to me now, but soon we developed a close friendship. He was the oldest of five children and the only boy. His personality was infectious. Steve was upbeat and jovial with an attitude that was definitely take-charge. He lived only a few blocks from the supermarket where I worked and our family shopped. About once a week, on days I wasn't working, I would drop my mother at the store to do our family's shopping then drive to the Talley house to hang out with Steve and his sisters until she was finished. Over time, his large family became the family I didn't have. Through him I experienced some of the pluses and minuses of having siblings, even though they weren't mine.

A group of four or five guys I knew from my new neighborhood, some of whom had tried out for and made the freshman basketball team, decided to bully me. Even in retrospect, I'm not clear why they thought I was such an easy mark. It started with intimidation for lunch money and continued for most of the fall semester. Finally, one day I'd had enough. On that day, the leader of the group, Mark Finnell, tried to shake me down for lunch money in the hall between classes. It was a bridge too far. I threw a punch at him. He blocked my fist with his notebook. Although he was bigger and probably stronger than me, he was so shocked I was standing up to him that he didn't retaliate. The bullying ended there.

Entering high school brought the idea of going to college into sharper focus. My parents made it clear they anticipated I would do as well at Shortridge as I had at School 32, despite the aforementioned challenges. My dad had a habit of comparing me to the children of his Jewish customers. Many times he told me the Jews reminded their children they had one strike against them because they were Jewish, so they must work extra hard to out-achieve the Gentiles. He would then add, "You have two strikes!" I was expected to achieve the same level of success as my Jewish contemporaries. From my adult perspective, I wince at the burden placed on my shoulders. But it was the 1950s, when doing what you were told was emphasized; it never occurred to me how difficult a task it might be. My father was such a dominant figure in my life that I hadn't developed the ability to question his directives. I simply tried to do as he wished.

NINE

WHY AM I SO FORTUNATE?

I WAS CURIOUS TO meet the new Mrs. Goodman. A few months after L.L.'s heart attack, I had the opportunity. I found Mildred was dramatically different from Esther. She displayed the aura of efficiency one might expect in a secretary. She spoke with a directness that paralleled her husband's, only with more subtlety. She was a few years younger than he was, plain in appearance, wearing little makeup, and dressed conservatively. They resided in a nice but much less stunning ranch-style house located in another upscale White neighborhood. I recall thinking the new house appeared a lot like Mildred: more conventional when compared to his previous one. The furnishings were nice but no longer lavish. The tiger rug was nowhere to be seen.

Mr. Goodman had expanded his pledge to me, perhaps because he had been forced to confront his own mortality. Shortly after he recovered from the heart attack, I learned he pledged to finance not only my college expenses but those for medical school as well. Plus, should he not survive to see me finish medical training, he would make sure his wife would honor his commitment to continue my support all the way to setting up a practice. Wow! My awe at his offer increased, as did my wonder over what prompted him to do this.

Once I began high school, my visits to the Goodmans' home most often occurred only at semester or vacation breaks. The first time I accompanied my dad to their new home, both greeted me warmly. L.L. usually asked, "How are you doing in school?" There were no stated GPA targets; I felt he simply expected me to do well academically. With his new wife, he seemed happier, smiling more often and sometimes exhibiting an almost jovial manner. His attire was more casual too, consisting now of sport shirts and slacks. On one visit, when the four of us were seated in the living room after my dad finished cutting his hair, I finally summoned the courage to ask my most burning question.

"Mr. Goodman, I am really grateful that you are planning to pay for my college and medical school education, but why are you are doing this for me?"

I was unprepared for his response.

"I am not doing this for you. I am doing it for Cal. I know he won't be able to afford to send you to college or medical school. Seeing you become a doctor is very important to him. We have been friends for a long time, and I want to do this for him."

Silence. Then I said, "I don't know how I can ever repay you."

"I don't expect you to repay me."

More silence as I pondered how to respond. The only words I could muster were "thank you!"

Mr. Goodman sometimes talked to my father and me about his two children. I encountered them from time to time as I was growing up. His son, Elliott, a professor at Brown University, was bookish and conservative in his manner, with glasses and a receding hairline. He resembled his dad, similar in height only slimmer. His daughter, Sue, was the opposite of her older brother. She was single and probably in her late thirties or early forties at this juncture. She was a little plump, but I thought her attractive; she constantly stressed over her looks. On the few occasions I recall seeing her, I felt her appearance seemed consistent with her personality: outgoing and talkative, upbeat and vivacious. She had short, cropped blonde hair and wore expensive, colorful, avant-garde, Southern California–style outfits. She spent a lot of her time in Los Angeles and Hollywood, connected in some fashion to the movie industry.

On one of our visits after I had asked why he'd made his pledge, Mr. Goodman told us about a comment that Elliott's son, who was about eight years old at the time, had shared with him: "My dad got a two thousand dollar discount on our new sailboat!" Then, pausing, looking directly at me, Mr. Goodman asked, "Considering the amount of the discount, how much do you think the boat must have cost?"

"A lot," I responded. I don't recall the figure, but it was several thousand dollars.

"Does it make you wonder how he could afford it on a professor's salary?" he asked me. "When Elliott was a youngster, he always wanted more than I provided him. At the time, I could meet his demands by simply working harder to increase my income. Now it is more difficult to do that."

In so many words, I understood Elliott still sought financial assistance from his dad. I think Mr. Goodman had become weary of providing it. I don't remember Sue coming up in the conversation, but from time to time, fragments of other conversations I overheard between L.L. and my dad spoke to his disapproval of what he considered her frivolous way of life. I surmised from these bits and pieces that while she was seeking to be part of the Hollywood celebrity scene, he was still supporting her too.

TEN

A SIXTEEN-YEAR-OLD BOY'S DREAM

GETTING A DRIVER'S LICENSE was the goal for every sixteen-year-old male, and it was no less true for me. On my sixteenth birthday, my dad took me to the state license bureau to take the written exam and the driver's test. I passed the written portion but, unexpectedly, failed the vision text, so I had to wait two or three additional weeks until I was fitted with glasses before I could return, complete the process, and get my first license.

Having a car in the late 1950s helped make you cool. The cooler the car, the cooler you were. Our family car was a 1955 Pontiac sedan. Big, heavy, and underpowered, it was by all measures a slug. But it became my first set of wheels when, somehow, my dad was able to purchase a used 1957 Mercury four-door sedan. "Almost as long as a Cadillac!" he often pointed out. In the 1950s, American cars were big machines with lots of sheet metal, chrome, and fins, so size and brand mattered. Cadillacs were at the top of the automobile food chain, the province of rich people and hustlers. Pontiacs, Buicks, and Mercurys were sort of in the middle, sandwiched between Chevys, Fords, and Cadillacs.

For a year, I enjoyed an increase in my coolness quotient now that I had wheels. But during the summer between my junior and senior years, the old Pontiac died. Kaput! Bumming a ride, public transportation, or borrowing my dad's Mercury were my only transportation options. After several weeks of my lobbying, my dad replaced the old Pontiac with a 1958 Chevrolet Impala coupe. The old Pontiac had around two hundred horsepower while the Chevy had over three hundred. Plus it was sleek and gold in color. My coolness index soared!

The same day as my trip to the state driver's license bureau, I began my first real job. It was as a stock boy in the supermarket where our family shopped since moving to our new home. Of course, my dad knew the store manager and arranged to have him hire me. The store was located about two miles from our house, situated along one of the routes I took when I walked home from school, so I knew it well. After confirming I was hired, I clearly remember Mr. Sullivan, the store manager, telling me to go home, put on a white shirt and a tie, then return to begin working. It was a typical hot, humid mid-June day in Indiana, but that didn't matter. My dad had already left, so I walked home as rapidly as I could, put on a shirt and tie, then hurried the two miles back to the store. Starting this job was a brand-new experience and totally exhilarating! Before this, my only income had been from periodically shining shoes for change on the sidewalk by our old apartment building while in grade school and cutting lawns with our push mower during summer vacations. All the other employees at the supermarket were White, and a couple of them were Southern Whites. I was the first Black employee. Working there broadened my horizons and increased my self-confidence more than I appreciated at the time. Until then, my social interactions outside school had been limited to individuals in my established circle. But the guys at the store were a different group altogether.

First, there was Lowell Sullivan, the store manager. Tall and thin, probably in his fifties, he had a deep voice belying his lack of bulk. With a personality that was reserved and a bit stern, he had a rather nervous manner, chain-smoked, and rarely made small talk. But when he spoke, you quickly learned to listen. Then there was Lloyd, the second man (first assistant manager). He had a similar physique to Mr. Sullivan; he was short and wiry, with an urgent intensity to his character. In his early thirties, he was much closer to my age and easy to be around. He was quite personable and particularly kind to me when I arrived.

Next was Bob, the second assistant manager. About the same age as Lloyd, he was tall and muscular, sort of a good ole boy type who, paradoxically, tended to have frantic moments belying his usual laid-back demeanor. There was Eddie, a stock boy like me but a couple of years older. Eddie had emigrated with his family from Poland. He was talkative and upbeat and spoke English with a pleasing Eastern European accent. He was the jester of the group, always making jokes and sometimes misunderstanding or misinterpreting our English idioms and clichés, which made him all the more funny.

Last was Al, the Italian American produce manager. He was probably about the same age as the store manager. Like most of the rest of us he was slender but shorter than me. Generally soft-spoken with an East Coast accent diluted from his years in the Midwest, he was playful and full of laughter, with a twinkle in his eye and an easygoing manner. His only flaw seemed to be his lack of assertiveness. I'm not sure why I remember this, but I felt he didn't receive the level of respect I thought he deserved. Notably, he and I were the only ones who didn't smoke. During my tenure a few others came and went, but this was the core group.

Curiously, given the time, the location, and the fact that I was the first Black employee in the store, there were only infrequent traces of racial prejudice. I remember only the rare racially tinged joke or cliché. When one of those occasions occurred, I wondered if the person who said it simply viewed me as another White member of the team or forgot I was there. I didn't perceive the comments to be malicious, just insensitive, such as saying "there's a nigger in the woodpile" if something seemed out of place. I chose not to object, but I can't say whether my reticence came from fear of rejection or the legacy of Jim Crow and not rocking the boat. However, while there were pranks typically played on new employees, such as being sent to find the can shrinker when the last can in the carton wouldn't fit on the shelf, I don't recall suffering any direct racial slurs. On the job, race didn't arise as an issue. My coworkers accepted me in the work environment and made me welcome as a member of the team, but not so surprisingly, at the end of the workday we went our separate ways. We did not socialize outside of the store; I can't recall that possibility occurring to me or ever coming up in our conversations.

There was, however, an exception. It was through them I learned about fast cars, drag racing, and automobile pinstriping, which is painting designs on a car as a means of customizing it. A guy called Little Al drove around the city following a circuit, making himself available to pinstripe your car on the spot. You had a general idea what day and about what time he would drive by looking for business. Needless to say, it was strictly cash and carry, so if you wanted some work done you needed to be ready with money in hand.

The street in front of the grocery store had a slight upgrade with only one side-street intersection over roughly a quarter-mile stretch. It wasn't a perfect strip, but it was good enough for drag racing. On Saturdays we cleaned the store after closing it at 10:00 p.m., generally finishing around midnight. We staged the races after that. The number of racers varied. Of course, our races weren't a secret, so the police would occasionally also turn up. When a squad car appeared, you would hear someone yell, "Cops!" then the laying of a lot of rubber as the racers scattered in all directions. A few times I was behind the wheel. As hazardous and illegal as the races were, they were really fun!

Working with the guys at the supermarket and being accepted by them was a big step. Years later, after finishing medical school, I worked as a volunteer physician at the Indianapolis Motor Speedway. At the track one day, as I walked along the fence toward the parking lot, I encountered Mr. Sullivan. Retired from the store, he was moonlighting as a gate guard during the racing season. It had been several years since we'd last seen one another.

"Hello, Lester!" he said. "How are you, and how have you been doing?"

Surprised, I responded, "Hi, Mr. Sullivan! It's good to see you again. It has been a long time." I spent a few minutes filling him in on what I'd been doing since I'd left the store. The brief conversation was an unanticipated role reversal. I had always looked up to him, and now he was reaching out to me.

Before I started driving, my dating activities bordered on nonexistent, but having a car changed all that. Driving didn't completely relieve my sense of awkwardness, but it helped. By my junior year, I had picked up a few more pounds and strategies that made me more confident around girls. Still, try as I might, I never had a girlfriend, just girl friends. Yet by the time I finished high school, I had learned a few important lessons about life, particularly how to deal with individuals and situations outside my customary world. My father continually emphasized the importance and benefits of being able to adjust to whatever situation confronted you. A big component of that skill was—as evidenced by his relationship with Mr. Goodman—the ability to communicate with anyone, no matter his social station or ethnicity, and to treat everyone as an equal even though it would not always be reciprocated.

ELEVEN

JUNIOR VAUDEVILLE

BY THE TIME I left School 32, the number of White classmates had diminished to the point that I had little opportunity to communicate with others unlike myself until I began working at the supermarket. As the racial balance at Shortridge shifted, socialization between Black and White students outside the classroom remained limited. This was most apparent in school-sponsored social activities. Excepting athletics, a few afterschool clubs, choral groups, and proms, the Black students generally didn't participate in school-sponsored activities such as dances and homecoming festivities. Interactions with my White and Jewish classmates were mostly superficial.

Each year the junior class put on an event called Junior Vaudeville. The show featured several skits produced by different groups of students. Neither I nor any of my friends of color had ever been to a performance, much less participated in a skit. The leaders of the in group decided it was time we changed that. A sponsor was found and we developed an act. Crafting the skit required a great deal of planning and hard work. We enlisted our entire community—parents, relatives and ministers—to help with planning, designing, making costumes, and choreographing. My inclusion confirmed to me that I had made it into the in crowd. There were two performances; on both nights our skit went smoothly. At the conclusion of the second night's performance the leaders of each skit, three girls for each group, took to the stage and were presented with a bouquet of roses by one of the members of their troupe.

That is, all but one group: ours. No one, not our sponsor (who was White) nor anyone else, had informed us about this tradition. We didn't know. The pain and embarrassment of our three leaders were palpable. Some of the sting lingers to this day.

TWELVE

SAYING GOODBYE AND A GLIMPSE OF MY FUTURE

IN 1961, I FINISHED high school the same way I started it: midyear, in January. Many of my friends had graduated the previous June and enrolled at IU's main campus in Bloomington. Since I had already played the starting-at-midyear scene at Shortridge, I did not want to repeat it by going to Bloomington in January. Mr. Goodman and my folks agreed to my request to take a couple of evening courses at the university extension (now a regional campus) in Indianapolis, maintain my job at the grocery store, and then matriculate to Bloomington in the fall. My eighteenth birthday fell on our June commencement day.

A few weeks after beginning classes at the extension, one of the most traumatic events of my life occurred. In jarring fashion, it introduced me to a world I would become intimately familiar with in a few years.

Elsie was four years my senior, but despite the age difference, we had been friends for as long as I could remember. Our mothers were close friends. Elsie also attended the IU extension with a class the same night as one of mine. Both classes ended at the same time. We didn't live far apart, and I often gave her a ride home. One particular night, I gave her a ride as usual. Later, while watching the eleven o'clock news, my mother shrieked when she learned a young woman had been shot and was in critical condition at Marion County General Hospital. It was Elsie.

John, Elsie's older brother, was a hothead with a temper like the flame in a butane lighter. After I had dropped her off, the two of them had gone to the home of a mutual friend. Once there, John and the friend argued. When the exchange became increasingly heated, John suddenly left, only to return a short while later armed with a pistol. The argument resumed and escalated to the point that John drew the gun, aimed it at his antagonist, and pulled the trigger. Elsie tried to intervene. She leaped in front of John's intended victim as he fired and was hit in the head.

My mother and I rushed to the county hospital to be with her parents, joining a group of Elsie's friends there. Some of them had already given blood donations for her. The night was doubly depressing not only because of why we were there but because the surgery waiting room of the old hospital was cold, poorly lit, and filled with strange sounds and smells as well as the muted conversations of the others there with us. Time seemed to flow like cold molasses as we waited for any news.

After what felt like an eternity, one of Elsie's doctors walked through the doorway leading from the surgical suites. His slow cadence and somber expression gave us the news before he spoke. Approaching Elsie's parents, he said softly, "She didn't make it." I remember thinking, "What inner strength do you have to have to be able to give that kind of news to a family?" At seventeen years of age, I struggled to find any words of comfort for Elsie's parents as tears began to flow. Nothing came except "I'm so sorry." Processing the knowledge that a person I had known almost all my life and left just a few hours earlier was now dead was difficult and excruciatingly painful. I had no clue that in only a few years, as a medical student, this building, now so foreign, would become very familiar to me. Had I given any thought to that possibility that night, the prospect would have seemed light-years away.

John was arrested, tried, and convicted of involuntary manslaughter. He served several years in prison.

Year One

1961–1962

THIRTEEN

YOUR MAMA DOESN'T LIVE HERE ANYMORE

THOUGH I WAS TAKING classes at the IU extension in Indianapolis during the spring, college didn't seem real until I arrived in Bloomington in September. In the early 1960s, Indiana University's main campus had approximately sixteen thousand students. Not counting foreign exchange and graduate students, three hundred to four hundred of us were Black.

In contrast to life in Indianapolis, the Indiana University campus was a tolerant oasis where the burden of racial segregation was partially lifted. Nevertheless, like every oasis, it had boundaries. Despite our newfound freedom, the specter of race never completely disappeared. It abided like an uninvited houseguest who did not often make his presence known, but when he did, you were obliged to take notice. Our parents had conditioned us to respond to racist encounters in a low-key manner typical of our generation. Nothing else compelled me to follow this course of action. At the outset, my interactions with my White classmates were similar to those in high school: generally cordial but superficial. The first years of the 1960s were what I now consider a transition period for my generation, sandwiched between the years of our parents' acquiescence to segregation and the activism of the civil rights and anti-war movements in the latter half of the decade. We were socially aware, but most of us had not risen to activism.

Despite many obstacles, Black students had a long presence at IU. The first African American to graduate from IU was Marcellus Neal in 1895. The athletic teams were integrated as early as 1892 when Preston Eagleson joined the football team. It was not until 1949, however, that IU star running back George Taliaferro became the first Black player drafted by the NFL. The men's dormitories were desegregated in 1947, with the women's dorms following shortly afterward. Yet the reality of race was apparent in student social interaction.

With such a small number of persons of color, we came to know each other well and developed relationships that would mirror those of students on historically black college and university (HBCU) campuses. By and large, we socialized with each other rather than with our fellow White students. The hub for most of our activities was the Indiana Memorial Union Building. The IMU is a massive, gothic structure that, then as now, contained not only guest rooms but several ballrooms of various sizes where dances were held. It also held the university bookstore, a bowling alley, a billiards room, a barber shop, and an upscale restaurant that most of my friends and I could not afford to patronize. Most important to us was its snack bar, called the Commons, where we gathered before, in between, and after classes. Because of its role as a social center and our small number, on any given day an explosion there would have wiped out the majority of the undergraduate Black student population.

I arrived on campus in late summer like almost every other freshman: driven there by my parents. It was still quite hot. The air was muggy on that Sunday afternoon, but for me it was also filled with apprehension and excitement. I realized I was standing at the threshold of adulthood, away from home and completely on my own for the first time.

Which university I would attend wasn't important to my parents. A chance visit to the Indiana University Bloomington campus as a thirteen-year-old high school freshman had set the stage for me. It was a sunny Sunday in the early spring when my mother and I accompanied my friend Fay and her parents on her trip back to the Bloomington campus. As we walked through the Kirkwood Street entrance, I felt like Dorothy reaching Oz in search of the wizard! All that was missing were Toto and Dorothy's companions. The red brick and limestone buildings in the central campus, the pedestrian footpaths winding their way through its abundant green space, the massive IMU, and the students, particularly the college girls, beguiled me. The place seemed almost magical. From that moment, college for me had meant IU.

This time, as we entered the campus, my head was swirling with a list of activities, including finding the admissions office and locating my dorm. My dormitory, Wright Quadrangle, completed in 1949, was so huge it required a map of its interior for the three of us to locate my room. Of course, meeting my roommate, unpacking the car, and carrying all my stuff into the room were the next orders of business. My mother, as the mother of an only child, began to direct me where to put my stuff. My roommate introduced himself then left the three of us alone.

My dad stood quietly in the room, probably worried what would happen to me now that I was beyond his reach. Possibly he contemplated how different his life would have been had he been able to go to college. My father's older sister, Frances, was the only family member to have obtained a bachelor's degree. She was the oldest sibling and, according to my dad, was treated as the shining star of the family. Aunt Frances had attended the segregated Nashville public school system through high school. Good fortune had provided financial aid and encouragement from a friend and mentor leading to a scholarship to Massachusetts College of Art and Design; she was one its first Black female students. She later earned a master's degree from Radcliff. My father placed the weight of his dreams squarely onto my shoulders. It was my mandate to make them come true.

While my mother busily doled out advice, with a list of what I will call the "be sure to's," I remember assuring them both I would be fine, though I was less certain than I tried to sound. As the afternoon moved toward evening, it was time for goodbyes. In their faces I saw a trace of sadness as they prepared to leave.

As I watched them go, the little bit of heaviness in my heart soon changed to anxious curiosity over what was to happen next. Despite all the emphasis on getting there, college had existed only as a word. Until the afternoon waned and my parents left for home, I had no clue what it actually meant. On this, my first day, I had all the trepidations and insecurities typical of any entering freshman. The mundane tasks were straightforward, but I had to figure out what to do after that. Picture this: all your life you've been told where to go, what to do, when to start, and when to finish. Now you are confronted with the reality that all of this no longer applies. Though help is available, it's completely up to you to seek it out. Your mama doesn't live here anymore!

My first roommate, Erastus Jason Miriti, was twenty and a sophomore. He was African, tall and skinny like me but with rather unkempt hair and a scruffy goatee. More specifically, he was a Kikuyu from a village near Nairobi, Kenya.

Until that day, I had never met anyone from Africa. Television newscasts and my high school international relations class had provided me with general information about Kenya and its ongoing struggle for independence from Great Britain. I was familiar with the names of its most prominent leaders, such as Jomo Kenyata and Tom M'boya. However, beyond that I knew almost nothing about the country and the rest of the continent. A good deal of what I had learned of Africa came from 1950s television shows consisting mainly of Black actors grunting "Sahib" and "Bwana" in the *Ramar of the Jungle* series or in the reruns of old Tarzan of the Apes movies from the 1930s and 1940s. Since Erastus—known as Jason—was from a village, I asked him, "What is it like to live in a jungle?"

Jason found my limited knowledge pretty comical. When he finally stopped laughing, he asked, "What do you mean by 'jungle'?"

"Out there on the savannas where the lions, zebras, and wildebeests roam free. What's it like living among them?"

"They are all in preserves."

"I wasn't referring to those in preserves but all the rest of them."

"There is no 'all the rest of them.' They are all in preserves. Didn't you know that?"

"No, I didn't."

"You don't know anything about Africa, do you?"

Again, I didn't, but I grew up a little that day.

After we moved beyond those preliminaries, we bonded well. I learned Jason had a zany personality. He laughed a lot. Annoyingly, he also developed the habit of calling me "kid" instead of Lester. With his British / Kenyan-accented English, it sounded like "keed." Despite my protests, he kept using this nickname until I finally gave up trying to change him. Notwithstanding how well we got along personally, I quickly realized we didn't have a lot in common, largely because he was two years older and considerably more worldly and mature than me. We continued as roommates for the remainder of the semester, but after the first couple of weeks we rarely went out together. He had little interest in my world and most of those who populated it. Sadly, he taught me very little about Kenya. I can't remember if it was a consequence of my lack of interest or his. He had his established group of friends, and I was still developing mine. When I informed him I decided to join a fraternity, he confessed he didn't know much about the Greek system but was unimpressed, figuring it was mostly elitist bullshit. To his credit, in retrospect, a fair amount of it was. Despite our differences, we kept in touch after we left Bloomington until I lost contact with him in the early 1980s.

Mr. Goodman kept his promise and not only paid my tuition but provided the funds for my books and housing fees as well. My parents were able to supply me with spending money. I established my first checking account and managed to get by on $5 to $10 a week! My dad and I saw Mr. Goodman at the end of each semester, to review the number of credit hours and costs for any additional fees, books, housing, etc. He also questioned me about my grades.

There was a formal freshman orientation program at the beginning of the semester; freshman arrived on campus a few days before the sophomores and upperclassmen. During those three days our counselors provided us with information about the courses we needed to meet the requirements of our first year of studies and how to register for them. The process of scheduling classes was daunting and, to most of us, chaotic. It was very different from the present when everything is online.

To register the entire student body required several days. The old basketball fieldhouse located in the central portion of the campus was the registration site. Each of us was given a specific day and time to arrive. Upon entering the cavernous building, you joined a huge crowd of noisy students all there for the same purpose. The room was filled with tables, each one representing a course; there was a line in front of every table. The goal was not only to sign up for the proper course but to get it at a specific time in your daily schedule. You may have also heard that it would be advantageous to have a certain instructor, so you tried to arrange that as well. In order to balance the sizes of the classes, enrollment in a course would be periodically suspended for a few minutes or considerably longer. If you were already at the table when the course closure was announced, you pleaded with the registrar to let you in before closing it. The effort rarely worked. If you were farther back in line, you had the option of simply waiting there, hoping it would reopen soon, or heading to another table to sign up for a different class, all the while keeping an eye on the table you just left so you could swiftly return to the line once it reopened. I'm still amazed the system actually worked, but it did. Somehow I managed to get the courses I needed at the times I wanted them.

Once I completed registration, bought my books and other supplies, learned the locations of my classes, and settled in with my roommate and the other guys on my dorm floor, I began pondering how I would navigate my way through this new world. Excepting Jason and myself, the rest of the men on my dorm floor were White. As a consequence, I remained a little apprehensive despite the relatively liberal racial climate on campus; I was, after all, in southern Indiana. Interacting with the other guys in my dorm unit on a daily basis, I found most were cordial. Our conversations were typically brief and superficial, rarely progressing beyond "hello" and "where are you from?" My prior experience with my workmates at the supermarket had been positive, so I didn't anticipate any serious problems with these guys.

Frustrated after receiving only a grade of C on my first English Composition paper, I lamented my situation and realized I needed to decide on a topic for the next essay. The assignment was to write a position paper to argue for or against a subject. I happened to discuss the assignment with Tom, one of my White unit mates. He told me he also had to do a paper on the same topic for the same course, and it was due soon. I asked what topic he chose.

"Segregation," he replied.

"Are you arguing for or against it?"

"For," he responded. "States' rights!"

"States' rights" was a recognized Southern code phrase used to rationalize maintaining racial segregation. I was taken aback and didn't challenge him, but my reaction must have revealed my shock. Later that evening, he appeared at my door to apologize for his answer. Integration, he stated, was really what he believed in, and he was very sorry for what he had said. I don't know if his apology was sincere, but I accepted it and told him so. What was likely his Freudian slip stayed with me for a while, but I appreciated he was empathetic enough to seek me out and apologize. Racism, however subtle, had not disappeared.

Besides getting into medical school, I had no clear road map for my time in Bloomington. I knew I did not want my undergraduate years to be a super version of high school. I discovered, as is usually the case, that a lot of life just happens. At the outset of your first semester, you don't yet declare a major. Nevertheless, the question is often asked. A lot of us answered "premed" in September. By the time first semester grades were in, many of the "premed" majors had shifted to "undecided." I didn't anticipate that a number of my friends would have difficulty getting a passing GPA. Enter another lesson from the real world.

FOURTEEN

OKAY, IT'S SHOWTIME!

ONCE CLASSES STARTED, THE process of adjusting to and assimilating into college began to come together. Officially, the university campus was dry, though drinking was pretty common. The unofficial watering hole for a lot of us was a place off campus in Bloomington, located on Seventh Street in the heart of the city's Black neighborhood. Its official name was the Pollard Elks Lodge, but it was nicknamed the Hole. The building was a basement covered with a roof. Why a house was never constructed over the foundation remains a mystery. The sole entrance was located at the bottom of a front stairway. The door had a small a sliding panel, like a 1920s speakeasy. Once you knocked, someone inside opened the panel and asked what you wanted. Unless you were a regular, you would have to flash an ID at him (it didn't always have to be yours) and usually he let you in. Inside there was a single large room with a bar, tables, a jukebox, and enough space for dancing. On weekends a few of the local regulars drank with us college kids. They were all "old" Black men who usually remained at the bar watching the young girls. We recognized some of them as deacons we'd see on Sunday mornings at Second Baptist.

The most important course for first-year premed students was Chemistry 101. My professor was Dr. Fredrick C. Schmidt. I remember his full name because that is how he introduced himself on the first day of class. When he pronounced his surname, you learned not to stand too near because "Schmidt" was often accompanied by a spray of saliva. Dr. Schmidt was a caricature of a college professor. He stood about five foot six, with an oval face, thick cataract-lensed glasses, and a shock of white hair that appeared as though it hadn't seen a comb recently. He wore tweed sport coats with elbow patches and smoked a pipe, though he forbade smoking in the lecture hall. On day one he wrote a phrase on the blackboard in German, translating it for the class:

"*Zu rauchen ist verboten!*" Literally, "to smoke is forbidden" or "no smoking."

Dr. Schmidt had a habit of pausing in the middle of a lecture to throw out a question to the class. He had a booming voice and didn't need to use a microphone.

"Ten points on the next exam to anyone who can answer this question."

Mind you, there were easily two hundred students in the lecture hall. This sounds like a good tactic, except for one little detail. Dr. Schmidt had several favorite students in the class whom he exclusively called on. Fortunately, I was one of them. Periodically, he would also pause during a lecture and tell a dirty joke. When this became a consistent pattern, several of the female students were offended and planned a demonstration to protest the next time he told another off-color joke. Their strategy was to stand and silently walk out of the hall. However, Dr. Schmidt had spies in the class who told him about the plan. A few days after learning of it, he stopped mid-lecture and uttered this statement: "I hear there is a shortage of prostitutes in New York City."

Immediately, perhaps fifteen women stood up, turned, and walked up the aisles toward the exit. Dr. Schmidt waited a few seconds, then followed up with this: "Wait, the next plane doesn't leave for three hours!"

The women were stymied. The class broke into raucous laughter. It was a terrible thing to do, blatantly sexist and terribly misogynistic. Today his insensitivity would not be tolerated. However, in 1961 it didn't matter. The attempted walkout fizzled and failed to alter his behavior. There were no further protests that semester.

To complete my degree required two years of a foreign language. I chose German. I wish I could remember why, but I don't. I'm not aware of any German heritage; it had nothing to do with Dr. Schmidt. My first instructor, Herr Gerlach, was a native speaker. Though I would not have employed the term then, he was stereotypically Teutonic—that is, very by the numbers in his teaching technique. Standing rigidly erect at just under six feet, he was likely in his mid-forties, very disciplined in his manner and speech but pleasant. I don't recall him smiling very frequently. On a few occasions, some of us met with him after class; during one of those sessions he shared a bit about his background. Since World War II had ended only sixteen years earlier, we asked him about his experiences in Germany during the war. Among other things, he mentioned he had been a member of the Hitlerjugend or Hitler Youth. We were shocked into silence! After an awkward pause, someone asked him, "Why did you join?"

He responded without showing any emotion. "It was a requirement for boys my age."

We had more questions. "What did you do there?" was the next one. In what was likely a bit of revisionist history, he replied that he functioned like a squad or a platoon leader; all he and his charges did was drill and sing. He was then asked if he knew about the concentration camps. I remember he looked perturbed when he said, "No." Some of us knew that as Germany was crumbling at the end of the war, essentially all boys over thirteen were given weapons and expected to defend the Fatherland. Boys had to be fourteen years old to join, so he would have been in that group. He told us he was never involved in any fighting. After these questions, the discussion ended. The irony is striking: me, a young Black man whose college education was being financed by a Jewish patron, studying German and being taught by a man who might be a former Nazi.

After five semesters, I was able to speak and read German reasonably well, but I didn't know anyone who spoke the language to be able to maintain proficiency. Still, I was able to employ it in a surprising situation a few years later. During medical school, I was asked to guide an undergraduate student from Brazil around the medical center. He spoke poor English, and I spoke no Portuguese. So why was I asked to show him the campus? I had listed German as the language that I had studied as an undergraduate as part of the application paperwork for medical school. He also spoke German. Luckily, I was able to resurrect enough of the language to converse with him. During the tour we happened upon one of my classmates. I introduced our visitor to him. When I explained why I was asked to be his guide, my classmate began speaking to him in perfect German! Go figure.

FIFTEEN

WHAT'S YOUR NAME?
WHERE ARE YOU FROM?

SURE, MY FELLOW STUDENTS and I attended classes and studied hard, but those activities didn't take up all of our time. Away from home and on our own for the first time, we delighted in being together. Our hub was the Commons. We played games of bid whist and bridge. We consumed loads of burgers and fries. The anticipation of falling in love was constantly in the air. Romances began and faded. At any given moment, it seemed everyone was part of a couple. Away from the Commons, we spent hours talking on the phone. There were study dates, strolls along the tree-lined footpaths, Greek parties, and dances. Almost every weekend someone brought a record player and a stack of records into one of the dormitory lounges, which generated a spontaneous party—a little "set," we called it. Thus, it is no wonder so much of my focus was devoted to social endeavors.

A review of my journal entries reveals a determination to be much more socially savvy than I'd been in high school. It was a new day—the slate was clean! To that end, I spent lot of my time and effort looking for love, at least the way an eighteen-year-old male college freshman would define it. Initially, this was not a quest for a lofty storybook romance. It was much more mundane. Label it old-fashioned physical lust, hopefully leading to getting laid. As crass as the that description may sound, it was the truth. Testosterone levels were soaring!

Perhaps surprisingly, neither I nor most of my close friends had been sexually active during high school. As odd as it may sound today, to us the term *making love* did not mean having sex. Most often it meant making out rather than getting it on. I quickly became aware of a couples' ritual one of my buddies called "acting like the world was about to end," later shortened to "ending the world." The female students had hours, meaning they had to be back in their dorms by eleven o'clock on weeknights and one o'clock in the morning on Friday and Saturday. Between fifteen and thirty minutes before "hours," couples would congregate in the area around the women's dormitory entrances and make mad, passionate love. The closer the clock ticked to closing time, the more intense the lovemaking became. This experience was totally new to me, but as time progressed I tried to take as much advantage of it as I could.

One of the first girls I met was Sandy Brown. Like me, she was an only child and a freshman. I first encountered her in the Commons because it seemed she was always there. About five foot five, she was shapely, with an oval face, deep brown eyes, and an olive complexion, and she was very talkative. Though the term had not yet been coined, she was the first assertive woman my age I had met. If it was a shovel rather than a spade, a shovel is what she called it! I was both intrigued and intimidated by her. She seemed to take an interest in me, because she said "yes" when I asked her out. I didn't record precisely what we did, but I remember we had a lively conversation as we strolled around the campus that warm fall evening. Understand, I was no great Romeo, so when we returned to her dorm the paramount question on my mind was whether to kiss her good night. When we reached the entrance of the building, though other couples were seriously making out, because I was uncertain how she would respond, I didn't try.

After our date, I knew I liked Sandy, but I didn't know what to do about it. We saw each other almost daily in the Commons, at a set at one of the dorm lounges, or at a party. A couple of my buddies confided to me that she'd told them she also "liked" me. However, she hadn't said that to me. Three weeks into the semester, the relationship had not moved in my favor, so I told her about my feelings. She responded that I was "one of many" guys in whom she had an interest. My pride wouldn't let me be "one of many," which I equated to standing in line. Despite my failed romantic effort, eventually we became good friends. She didn't forget how our first date ended because years later she told me, half in jest and half in annoyance, that when we'd said good night, "You patted me on the back and kissed me on the cheek." It was not the way to kindle a romance.

Harold Thompson was one of the first persons of color I chanced upon when I arrived on campus. Meeting him served up another lesson in daily living, demonstrating that people, like things, are not always what they seem. Because of our shared surname, we were placed in the same freshman orientation class. He and I were the only Black students. Initially, we didn't relate at all well to each other. Harold, who later became known as Bookie, was short, about five foot seven, and dressed like a hood. In high school, then as now, your attire often reflected what group you belonged to. He wore a long-sleeve, cotton-knit collared shirt with high-waisted trousers and Cuban boots. By contrast, I was used to wearing blue jeans (this was long before they were considered fashionable) and a plaid work shirt with sneakers. I thought he was a gangster; he thought I was a country bumpkin. He was surprised to learn I was also from Indianapolis. Although we shared the same hometown, we had attended different high schools.

Before the end of the orientation session, we did reach out to each other. Once we began to connect, we learned how wrong our first impressions were and to be skeptical of future first impressions. We joined the Scrollers, Kappa Alpha Psi Fraternity's pledge class, together and underwent initiation in the same line or group, and we have remained close friends to this day.

SIXTEEN

WHAT'S A GREEK?

AS MY CAMPUS LIFE began to develop, I became exposed to the world of the Black fraternity and sorority or Greek system. My social life was often coupled with fraternity life. By the end of the first week of school, it became clear if I wished to have the best social life, I needed to join a fraternity.

The social structure of the student population at Indiana University was functionally divided into those who belonged to the fraternities and sororities (the Greeks) and all the rest, the GDIs (god damned independents). Greek organizations on campus were effectively divided into three groups: Whites, Blacks, and Jews. There was little mobility between the three. The country's first academic fraternity, Phi Beta Kappa, was founded shortly after the publication of the Declaration of Independence. However, it was not until the early nineteenth century that strictly social fraternities were established.

Black Greek organizations did not exist until after the turn of the twentieth century. I was told our founders as well as many of the others who had started Black Greek organizations learned about rituals and practices while working in White fraternity and sorority houses in the late nineteenth and early twentieth centuries. Alpha Phi Alpha, founded at Cornell University in 1906, has been credited as the first African American fraternity; Alpha Kappa Nu Greek Society was established at IU in 1903 but lasted only two years. Within the next decade, the Omega Psi Phi Fraternity and the Alpha Kappa Alpha and Delta Sigma Theta sororities were established at Howard University. Alpha Kappa

Nu fraternity was succeeded by Kappa Alpha Nu at Indiana University in 1911. In 1915, Kappa Alpha Nu's name was changed to Kappa Alpha Psi primarily because the last Greek letter was being used as a racial slur: Kappa Alpha "Nig." By the time I arrived, all five of these existing Black Greek organizations had IU chapters. I knew nothing about any of them.

Every college fraternity and sorority has a mission statement professing lofty goals, usually of brotherhood or sisterhood, community service, and scholarship. Though each of the Black Greek organizations at IU made some effort toward putting those lofty aspirations into practice, most of what we did had little to do with community service. It consisted primarily of enjoying the status of being a member of a select community and punching a ticket to a good time. I can speak only about my fraternity, the Kappas, during my tenure at IU. Over the past sixty years, the national organization and the local chapters have made great strides toward fulfilling the Kappa Alpha Psi mission statement: to promote spiritual, social, intellectual, and moral welfare.

At IU, each Black Greek organization had a distinct reputation. Among the fraternities, the Alphas were thought of as intellectuals, the smart guys. In contrast, the Kappas were viewed as party boys and hell-raisers. The Omegas, also referred to as the Q's, were perceived to land somewhere between the other two. By their nature, these organizations were elitist. Not everyone who expressed an interest was allowed to join.

Despite some petty competitiveness, there was surprisingly little friction among the Black Greek organizations. Generally, we interacted cordially with one another and often partied together. On occasion, we Kappas did engage in social activities with other Greek organizations, but, excepting the AKAs and the Deltas, exclusively with the two Jewish fraternities and sororities. I don't recall cosponsoring any events with the White Greek chapters. Despite functioning in essentially separate worlds, there was no open hostility between "us and them." It was more a reflection of the Jim Crow world to which we were accustomed. Simply, they did their thing and we did ours. Except in the most general sense, I gave little if any thought to whether becoming a Kappa would contribute much to my path toward maturity or my future goals. However, it did in ways I did not anticipate.

By the time I arrived in Bloomington, several of my friends were already Kappa pledges, Steve Talley among them. I saw how the actives, the "big brothers" in the vernacular of the time, were admired and stood atop the social pecking order. There was a lot of talk about brotherhood and group cohesiveness, all for one and one for all stuff. There also was a level of friendly one-upmanship between the different fraternities and sororities, not limited to just the Black ones. The Kappa men considered themselves to be at the social pinnacle. Everyone wants to belong to something, especially if it is considered to be exclusive and exceptional. I quickly realized *everyone* included me. Since most of my friends were Kappas, coupled with my perception that, although they may have been party boys, the Kappas were still the coolest of the frats, I wanted to become a pledge, a Scroller.

My parents knew little about college fraternities. When I informed them of my plan to become a pledge, they voiced reservations about allowing me to do so during my first semester. I told them, falsely as it turned out, it would not involve a large amount of my time. With my urging they grudgingly agreed, with one caveat: my grades must not suffer. Mr. Goodman raised no objection when my dad broached the subject with him, given the same stipulation. I don't know how much involvement he'd had with the Greek system as a college undergraduate. However, his alma mater, Butler University, located in Indianapolis not far from where I'd lived during my teens, had a vibrant Greek scene. I suspect that was also the situation when Mr. Goodman was a student. He was a Mason, but as far as I can determine, he did not belong to a college fraternity.

It's hard to overstate the importance Greek life had for all of us. Becoming a Greek was a goal many of us sought for numerous reasons, not the least of which was because it would provide a pathway to higher social status. There was also prestige and what we now call networking. Once you became a pledge and subsequently were initiated into the group—"going over," as we called it—you felt as though you were on top of the world! At least, that was my experience.

Since almost all fraternities and sororities are in some measure secret societies, there was an overarching air of mystery as well as anxiety in seeking to be "worthy" enough to become a member. The Greek organizations usually recruited new members early in the semester at a get-together during campus Rush Week. For the fraternities, the event was generally referred to as a "smoker." The term was a literal one. Most often these recruiting sessions were held at the respective houses. None of the Black Greek organizations had a house, so the Rush Week activities were usually held in a conference room in the Union Building. Since smoking was common, it was permitted almost everywhere. During these events, the frats typically had their most prominent members in attendance for you to meet. They touted how great their organizations were and how you would certainly want to join them. It was very similar to the college recruiting process for a high school athlete. Once you signed a pledge card, you became a pledge. The second week of October, I became a Scroller.

Once you pledged you suddenly became a second-class citizen, always subordinate to the wishes of the big brothers. At fraternity events, that was how you addressed them, as Big Brother So-and-So. Greek life became an integral part of the pledges' day-to-day existence. It was like a garment you never removed. The fraternity affected to one degree or another how you behaved, with whom you became friends, and, often, the flow of your routine activities. Another significant facet of fraternity life was that you weren't assured of being initiated simply because you pledged. You were told you had to "earn" the "right." How to earn the right was never clearly explained. It was very much a play-it-by-ear process. If you screwed up too often, you might be held back when your pledge class or line was initiated or dismissed and "depledged." The actives were judge and jury.

Being a pledge also required a significant amount of time. Mostly it involved going to fraternity meetings—"board meetings," as they were called—and yes, the word *board* was not just a euphemism. Part of each fraternity's paraphernalia was a lacquered wooden paddle, often referred to as a board. The fraternity's crest and its name in large Greek letters were etched into the surface. Once initiated, each active was entitled to obtain one. The paddle was advertised as an artifact of the days when physical hazing of pledges was commonly practiced; however with the Kappas it was not only symbolic. Although hazing had been officially outlawed by the university as well as by the fraternities, in one form or another it persisted. There were also various other restrictions placed on your activities. Our meetings were typically held late Sunday afternoon or early Sunday evening in an IMU conference room, but a "special board meeting" could be called in one of the actives' rooms or one of his favorite outdoor spots, at any time without prior notice. The only valid excuse for missing one was you couldn't be located to receive the summons. Sometimes the topic on the meeting agenda was serious.

Right after our first-semester midterm exams were completed, a board meeting was called for the Scrollers to report their grades. The grade point average (GPA) of each fraternity and sorority was monitored by the university. A chapter falling below a passing GPA could be sanctioned; this was an important metric. We pledges were lined up in front of the seated actives. Each of us in turn was required to step forward and report his midterm GPA. I was fifth or sixth in line. As the process unfolded, the atmosphere in the room grew darker. It began to feel as though we were at a wake. Each pledge before me in line turned his gaze toward the floor as he stepped forward and mumbled out his average. Nobody had over a 2.0, and a couple had averages below that. I felt almost embarrassed to say I had a 3.0. Clearly, my commitment to academic achievement was far different from some of my fellow Scrollers. I wondered if the Scroller class's academic struggles were going to be a persistent problem. The answer was yes.

There could also be a lot of silliness at board meetings. At one we were lined up and told not to smile, no matter what. The actives did everything they could to make us to laugh without actually touching us. Inevitably, one of us could no longer restrain himself and broke. We were then instructed to drop down into a push-up position and wipe the smiles off our faces. I'd call it mild hazing—stuff intended to embarrass you while fostering a spirit of group unity, generally referred to as "brotherhood." Physical punishment for perceived wrongdoing remained a part of the picture, varying from what I just described to paddling at late-night board meetings. Despite what may seem like a slew of negatives, most of my time in the fraternity was actually fun. There was plenty of camaraderie and a magnetic group identity.

SEVENTEEN

A PEEK AT WHAT LIES AHEAD

A MONTH HAD PASSED since I became a Scroller, and my life at school was going well. I continued to spend time with my old and new friends after class and on weekends. One of the most important activities in the Greek year is initiating new members—the time when pledges become actives. The week leading up to the formal initiation, or going-over ceremony, is traditionally referred to as Hell Week. The Kappas labeled it Neophyte Probation or simply Pro. Those who were about to be initiated were called neophytes or probates. The entire group was referred to as a line.

As far as I could tell, most if not all the fraternities and sororities continued to engage in hazing of one sort or another. The Kappas were no exception. The reigning philosophy for Hell Week struggles was "if I went through it, you will too." Since my turn to go over would not arrive until the spring semester, I was relegated to being an observer. Suffice it to say Hell Week for the four neophytes was aptly named. It was a rugged time, not just for those four but, in a different sense, for the rest of us Scrollers. They were soon to become big brothers, and we weren't. Friday, the last night of probation, called "turn back night," was just what the label implies. There was always a question as to whether all the probates would endure the punishment and make it all the way through to the end.

Once the probates became actives, an unanticipated question arose: How would we, the remaining Scrollers, relate to our new big brothers until our turn came in the spring? A week earlier we had all been in the same situation as pledges. Now they had made it to the show, and we were still stuck in the minor leagues. I, along with a couple of other Scrollers, sought out the new actives the morning they were made. All of them looked maltreated, but once they became actives their tormentors suddenly became their compatriots. Their joy was palpable! At the completion of the initiation ceremony, which traditionally happened in the early morning hours on Saturday of Hell Week, they were congratulated by their new brothers as though their team had just won the big game and none of the events of the prior week had ever happened. I didn't know it then, but it's akin to having just completed basic training in the military. You have survived the struggle and earned the right to be a member of the team. To a degree, I shared their joy and their relief in making it through the process. We were happy to have aided their line in small ways to get through the week's ordeal. But, at the same time, it made me eager to experience the same thing without having to wait until the following spring.

EIGHTEEN

THE CLEAVERS OR THE BUNKERS?

THANKSGIVING BREAK WAS RAPIDLY approaching. I wasn't able to score a ride home, so I ended up taking a Greyhound bus from Bloomington to Indianapolis. We called it "hitting the Hound."

Thanksgiving Day and Christmas Day were special to me because they were two of the few times both of my parents and I shared a meal. We had no extended family close by. Rarely did my family entertain dinner guests, not even our neighbors in the building. We were seldom invited out.

As I recall those memories, it is clear we did very little as a family. My mother worked, and my father usually arrived home late, most often after my mother and I had eaten dinner. There was little conversation between them. Often, what conversations there were devolved into arguments about the family's finances. My father would then retire alone to the bedroom. Nonetheless, I looked forward to going home.

In the 1950s and 1960s, there were several family sitcoms with idealized households, including *Leave It to Beaver* and *Father Knows Best*. As children, many of my friends and I were fans of those domestic comedies we watched on television. We actually believed our families were like those portrayed on the screen. In reality, most were more like the Bunkers in the later sitcom *All in the Family* than the Cleavers in *Leave It to Beaver*.

NINETEEN

RAY CHARLES

THE WEEKS BETWEEN THANKSGIVING and Christmas break were taken up primarily with studying for my final exams, which were scheduled for late January. For the Christmas break, I was able to catch a ride home with Dave Thomason, a guy I did not know, but whose father was one of my dad's customers. Since I was without a car on campus, my father suggested I contact him to arrange the ride. I joined Dave and his dad in his dad's brand-new Oldsmobile. What made the trip notable was the story Dave's dad related to us. On the way, he provided details of Ray Charles's Indianapolis arrest.

Two years earlier, a relative of one of my cousins had slipped her, her sister, and me into a local venue where Ray was appearing. It was billed as a dance and show held in a skating rink we used to frequent in one of Indianapolis's Black neighborhoods. We were all underage and had no business being there, but our excitement was difficult to contain. The rink was packed with people talking, laughing, smoking, and drinking. Tables with setups were arrayed on the floor, leaving enough room for the little stage and dancing. It was BYOB; those with sufficient resources had a fifth of alcohol setting in the middle of their tables. The less well-off had only a half pint.

Starting at the designated time did not apply here. As the evening wore on without Ray making an appearance, the crowd became restless. There was no opening act, just Ray. After a long wait, applause erupted as he was led into the room and took his seat at an electric piano, which was a new instrument at the time. I'd never seen or heard one live. After playing a few bars, he paused, stared directly into the crowd, and from somewhere deep inside uttered a long, loud, guttural "yeaaaah!" and began to jam. The crowd exploded into cheers.

That Ray was a heroin addict was common knowledge. He was almost certainly high that night. It was common for rhythm and blues and jazz musicians in those days to abuse drugs, alcohol, or both.

A year later, when he had another gig in Indianapolis, he was arrested on a drug charge. Dave's dad had been the prosecutor on the case, and on the way home he gave us chapter and verse of what went down. According to Dave's dad, an anonymous tipster informed the police someone had delivered drugs to Ray's hotel room. The following day, the police entered his room, found the drugs, and arrested him. Allegedly, he confessed to being an addict. After being booked, he was released on bail. I had read the newspaper account, but it was fascinating to hear the details from the prosecutor. At Ray's arraignment a few months later, the charges were dismissed because the police had not identified themselves when they knocked on his hotel room door but stated they were delivering a telegram from Western Union. Ray beat the rap on that technicality.

The whole affair was far removed from my own experience. As far as I knew, none of my friends in high school had used drugs. As kids in my old neighborhood, we occasionally found drug paraphernalia in the alley; I don't recall ever witnessing anyone shooting up. We thought mainlining heroin was simply stupid. There was nothing glamorous about selling or using drugs. For my crowd, cigarettes and alcohol were the vices of choice.

TWENTY

A NEW LOW

BACK AT SCHOOL, WHEN I awoke on the morning of Wednesday, January 10, 1962, the temperature in my dorm room made me feel like I was standing outside. I was as cold as I had ever been.

"Jason, turn up the heat!" I told my roommate.

"There isn't any heat," he replied.

"What do you mean, there isn't any heat?"

The reason, Jason informed me, was the central heating plant that provided heat for most of the main campus buildings and many of the dorms, including mine, had crashed during the night. I asked him, "How cold is it?"

"Seventeen below zero!"

"What?"

He repeated it; this was the coldest day of the year and a record low. We had ice an inch thick on the inside of the window to complement several inches of snow outside. To make matters worse, I had a chemistry exam that morning that I could not afford to miss. Because there were so many freshmen on campus that semester, there were not enough classrooms available for every course. My chemistry class was held in the Von Lee Theater, located a block off campus. I had to get to class. So, after putting on almost all the clothes I had, I walked the mile or so from Wright Quad to the theater. It was brutal! There was one saving grace when I arrived: it was heated! By the end of the day, the power plant was back in service.

When first semester grades were posted, I managed only a C in Elementary Composition and B's in the remainder of my courses. I was disappointed to slip below my midterm 3.0 GPA but decided it wasn't too bad an achievement for my initial semester. Several of my friends had done less well. A visit to see Mr. Goodman during semester break went uneventfully. I think he considered my performance sufficient for an entering freshman. Yet I do not remember receiving any direct praise. Surprisingly, he never referred to his experiences in college. It led me to wonder how accomplished a student he had been.

TWENTY-ONE

SOMETHING REALLY SPECIAL

OUR FRATERNITY'S NATIONAL ORGANIZATION, the Grand Chapter, appropriated funds to build a chapter house to commemorate the fiftieth anniversary of its founding in 1911. Where to locate the house generated a contentious debate. A contingent of members from the South wanted it to be placed in one of the HBCUs, but since the fraternity had been founded at IU, the proponents of locating it there won the day. Construction was underway for months, with its completion date set at the start of the spring semester of 1962. During its construction, several of us would often visit the site to watch its progress.

One evening, a few days before leaving for winter break, I dropped by Steve's room. He was there with Wayne Payne. He looked at me and said, "Let's take a walk to the Kappa House!" After questioning the wisdom of walking two miles there and back on a cold December night, Wayne and I agreed to go along. The outbound leg was uphill. The three of us made it there without incident, but before we gained entry we had to shoo away a couple parked in the lot behind the house. Before we left his dorm room, I had asked Steve, "How are we going to get inside?" He'd told me he had been there earlier in the day and left a main floor window slightly open. When we arrived, we found the window locked. Luckily for us, there was a broken pane in another front window, which we squeezed through. Once inside, we began acting like silly little kids, running around turning on every light in the place. The workers had left the heat on, so we were comfortable to boot. After exploring its interior, we ventured back outside to admire the building with the lights ablaze. This visit stoked my desire to move in when it opened at the beginning of the spring semester.

The grand opening of the new Kappa Alpha Psi Fraternity house was quite an affair! The architect, the general contractor, assorted Grand Chapter officials, and many university administration officials were there for its dedication. Three of the surviving founders were also present. Of course, most of the African American students and a large number of the White and Jewish ones came to see the facility. Joan Stanton was one of them. She had just become an Ivy—an Alpha Kappa Alpha (AKA) Sorority pledge. The AKAs were functionally a sister sorority to us Kappas. We interacted often as a group and individually. By serendipity, Joan spent a good portion of the weekend at the house during the festivities. We were acquaintances and, until that weekend, nothing more. Observing how she moved among the myriad of visitors at the house, I discovered there was something special about her I had failed to notice. Animated and playful with just a hint of restraint, she was tantalizing beyond measure. I knew two other guys were already making moves on her, so initially I was reluctant to add my name to the list. But as the weekend unfolded and I spent more time around her, I began to rethink my decision. Winning her affection would not be easy, but by the end of the weekend I decided to throw caution to the wind and go for it. Sadly, Joan and I did not share any classes. However, a friend, Finnis Anderson, did. One day shortly afterward, I posed this question to him: "What is it like to sit in class with her?" His answer has remained with me: "Let's just say that I'm terribly aware of her presence."

Being the only Black Greek organization with a house, especially a brand-new one, was exceptional. We viewed it as such. Over the preceding few years, several of the White and Jewish fraternities and sororities had built new houses along North Jordan Avenue, dubbed Fraternity Row, each reportedly costing over $100,000. The Kappa House, as we called it, sitting at the north end of Fraternity Row, reportedly cost $100,000 (over $868,000 in 2020 dollars) to construct. It was a rectangular limestone building with three floors, designed for sixty occupants. Included among its features were a fireplace and a grand piano. I have no clue who decided to provide the piano, but it was a real asset at party time as several of the brothers could play. The dining hall was large enough to hold dances. Overall, the house was not only an attractive structure but a functional one as well.

I was in awe over the entire celebration and quickly agreed to move in with the initial group, after I convinced my parents and Mr. Goodman I could successfully manage myself and stay focused on my studies. Despite the glorious future a brand-new house would bring to the chapter, one important fact was left out: the occupants would be responsible for running and maintaining it. As part of the compromise in the agreement to build the house at IU, no funds for its maintenance would come from the national organization. It would have to be self-sustaining.

The university required each fraternity and sorority to have an adult, a house father or mother, available to oversee running the facility. Our guy was Freddie Stewart, a Kappa and Bloomington native who had finished his undergraduate degree several years earlier. He was in his mid- to late thirties and worked in the city. Steady and level headed with a calm demeanor, he was our "rock in a weary land." Freddie was a little guy, maybe five foot five, perhaps 145 pounds, but trim and muscular. He had a temper but rarely unleashed it. Often he was the one to whom we turned for counsel. Starting as a mentor, he became my valued friend by the time I left college. He was a devout Bahai—the first one I came to know. Until I met Freddie, I was not even aware of the existence of the Bahai faith.

Despite the presence of the new house, the chapter was unable to recruit a sufficient number of individuals to fill it. Because of low occupancy, it was decided that we would use only the first and second floors; the third floor would remain unoccupied. Two of us would share a study room; we would have our individual bunks in the second floor dormitory located at the western end of the building. My roommate, Gerald Adams, was another a freshman. We developed a sincere friendship, including going over in the same line of Scrollers.

Though we had a house father, day-to-day operations were left to us. Any sense of concern over that fact, which later became a serious issue, had yet to appear. Being a lowly pledge as well as a freshman, I believed the Grand Chapter and all the actives knew what they were doing and managing the new facility ourselves was the norm, though none of us had any prior experience in doing it. In order to maintain the building in good condition, we were instructed by the builder how to care for it. Chores were assigned to each of the pledges by Steve Talley, who assumed the role of house manager for weekly Saturday morning cleanup sessions. At the outset, things ran smoothly.

TWENTY-TWO

"I'M TERRIBLY AWARE
OF HER PRESENCE"

OVER THE TWO WEEKS following the open house festivities, my courtship efforts increased. I hoped it was the beginning of a romance. To my great joy, Joan and I started spending a lot of time together. There were times when I felt the effort was going my way. But there were equally as many when she demonstrated to me I was wrong. A big dance was set for a month after our open house. I wanted her to be my date but was unsure she would accept if I asked her.

It was uncharacteristically quiet in the second-floor dorm. I was not yet asleep. The only sounds were the muffled snores of a couple of the brothers. The glow from the exit sign above the back stairway door bathed the room in a verdant hue. Outside, a night sky full of stars welcomed the new moon.

"You have a phone call," Chuck, one of my pledge brothers, informed me.

As I eased myself out of bed and headed down the hallway to the phone, I muttered to no one, "Who in the hell is calling me on Thursday at midnight? Is it some crisis at home?" Half asleep, I picked up the receiver.

"Hello."

"Hello, Lester. This is Joan."

Joan? JOAN!

After a couple minutes of small talk, she told me why she had called. "If you don't have other plans, would you be my date for the upcoming dance?"

I was gleeful! Naturally, I replied, "Yes," all the while trying not to sound too eager. True to form, after hanging up, on my way back to bed, I began to second-guess my good fortune. Was her invitation a pledge duty? Was I was her last option for a date? I couldn't imagine any of her other suitors would turn her down. I decided it didn't matter. With the security of her as my date for the dance, I could spend more time devoted to catching up on my schoolwork and raising my GPA.

One of the petty psychological tools fraternities and sororities used to exert dominance over their pledges was called "social probation," or "social pro" for short. It could be sprung at any time, often just before the onset of the weekend. It consisted of placing a restriction on the pledges' social activities. For example, if you had a date, you couldn't keep it. Sometimes it was initiated because of a real or perceived infraction by one of the pledges, so all would suffer the same penalty—all for one and all that. At other times it was simply applied at the whim of the actives.

About five o'clock in the afternoon the day before the dance, there was a call for me. It was Joan. "I called to tell you that I won't be able to go to the dance with you tomorrow night," she said. Earlier in the day, one of my friends had told me he'd heard the Ivys were going on social pro the day of the dance. Often, when those restrictions were about to be put into effect, it was deemed a secret; if true, the Ivys were not supposed to acknowledge it. This ruse never made sense because word always leaked out. Joan didn't explain why she cancelled. Whatever the reason, our date was off. My self-doubt resurfaced. What had really happened?

One of my weaknesses at that juncture in my life was a great deal of wishful thinking. For weeks after the disappointment, I had conversations with myself pondering imaginary "what if" scenarios. There was no one I felt I could trust to confide in about my distress over the failed romantic pursuit. In high school, I'd read Dante's *Inferno*; in it, he imagined nine circles of hell. The first circle contained the virtuous pagans, those who had died before the coming of Christ and had not received baptism. Their only punishment was no hope of ever entering paradise. At the time I hadn't viewed it as such a severe sentence. But now, after a series of failed romances, I began to understand how painful having absolutely no hope can be. In matters of the heart, I often felt disadvantaged and awkward, the way a younger sibling might feel when failing to outdo his older brother. I believed romance was the culmination of a zero sum game: you won or you lost. I was not yet able to simply enjoy the journey. All the colors in my emotional palate were bold. There were no pastels or muted tones. Reflecting on those beliefs now, I see my focus as sexist and immature. Of course, to one degree or another, I was both.

TWENTY-THREE

IT'S MY TURN—OR IS IT?

AS WINTER YIELDED TO spring, my attention turned toward the upcoming initiation. My Scroller line was the next group to go over. The date for the beginning of every probation was supposed to be a secret, but it was never a well-kept one. Traditionally, the going over dance was held in Alumni Hall in the Union Building. To discover the date, all one had to do was drop by the scheduling office and peruse the schedule of events. The hall was reserved by the Kappas for March 17. Two weeks before the planned start of pro, daily life for us pledges, as we witnessed for the previous Scroller class, became more arduous, with more frequent hazing. As each day passed, the intensity escalated. With the arrival of March, we learned of an event that would prove prophetic.

The same night the hall was reserved for our dance, the great and mercurial jazz trumpeter Miles Davis and his band were scheduled to perform a concert in the IU auditorium, sponsored by the local NAACP chapter. We hoped it would not affect our dance. Having Miles appear at IU was a big event. Had the concert been scheduled for any other night, many of us would have planned to attend.

Four days before the start of Hell Week, the actives announced that the dance, which we were not supposed to know about, was cancelled at the request of the NAACP. We Scrollers collectively felt extreme disappointment and anger. To be released from the second-class shackles of being a pledge and become a full-fledged Kappa was our mission and our focus. Having those desires dashed, even for a few weeks, was devastating!

Viewing my reaction through the lens of time, it was understandable but immature and naive. The NAACP chapter certainly needed the financial support the concert would provide. Scheduling an appearance by Miles Davis was a lot more difficult than rescheduling our dance. But all that was lost on us. We were so angry, we agreed to boycott the concert. Ironically, it failed to happen; Miles canceled the day prior because of illness. It was never rescheduled. That made us even madder, but there was nothing we could do except wait for probation to be rescheduled.

TWENTY-FOUR

WHAT IN THE WORLD WAS THAT?

AT THE START OF the spring semester, a graduate student from Tennessee moved into the house. Hubert Crouch was a PhD candidate in the School of Health, Physical Education, and Recreation (HPER). With the exception of our house father, Freddie, he was the oldest of the actives. Generally quite mellow in his attitude and approach toward us Scrollers, his advice to us was simply, "Be humble and be cool." However, one day something happened. Suddenly he began acting bizarrely. The first example of his strange behavior was an edict he issued to two of the Scrollers. Without explaining why, he told John Jones and Vic Bender, a freshman football player and freshman basketball player, respectively, they had to be in bed and "sleep," not "asleep" but "sleep" (he was a southerner), by eight o'clock. Everyone treated this as joke. It wasn't. He was deadly serious. So visualize two hefty college athletes literally in bed by eight in the evening. The only resistance they could put forth was to complain. Once under the covers, they whined, "We don't want to go to bed, Daddy Crouch! Please don't make us go to bed!" Of course, all of us thought this was outrageously funny. That is, all of us but Hubert Crouch. He was infuriated!

After this opening gambit, it got worse. The following night at dinner, Crouch took away our napkins and said we were not to use any. Roger Birt, another one of the actives, contravened his decree and said we were to put them back and continue to use them. He and Crouch kept issuing conflicting orders to the pledges until finally we ignored Crouch and kept the napkins.

In the early morning hours of the next day, I was told Crouch had run out into the rain and ended up at the IMU to see Val Washington, saying as he left that he had a "personal problem." Val was in his sixties and a successful businessman in Washington, DC. He was an Indiana native, a distinguished IU alumnus, and the key individual in the Grand Chapter who was responsible for siting the house at IU. He remained in Bloomington for a month after the open house to assist us in managing it.

Later in the day, Crouch returned saying he had talked to four or five people about lodging a protest after the Kappa intramural basketball team lost in the semifinal game of the fraternity tournament, in part because of some questionable calls by the referee. He added, "Scared the hell out of them!" His wide-eyed, wildly disheveled appearance as he related his story supported what he told us. I could easily believe he did frighten whomever he spoke to!

None of us understood Crouch's bizarre actions. Most of us were confused and annoyed. I was angry but then began to feel sorry for him. Later the same night, he came to my study room looking sad and sick. He acknowledged he was sick, and he had to have his bed moved from the dormitory into his study room. I didn't ask why he approached me for help, but I agreed to give him a hand. His strange behavior continued for several more days until his father arrived and took him away. We never learned what happened to him, nor did we understand what had triggered his outlandish behavior. At the outset, when we'd learned he was not joking, some were afraid of him, and a few began to feel sorry for him, but in the end most of us thought he had gone crazy. None of us knew what the term actually meant. Now I believe he suffered delusions from acute schizophrenia. This was my second encounter with someone with an obvious mental illness. I didn't connect the two at the time, but some of his bizarre outbursts rang a bell in my memory: L.L. Goodman's wife, Esther.

TWENTY-FIVE

LET'S TRY THIS AGAIN

RUMOR HAD IT OUR initiation dance was rescheduled for one month after the original date, which meant probation would start at the beginning of that week. The first week of April brought on the onerous pledge duties. We were instructed to beg the actives for additional assignments. There were tasks to perform, such as shining the actives' shoes or running their errands. I suppose these were measures designed to reinforce group cohesiveness. That might be a generous interpretation.

Hell Week began on Monday. All of us took an oath not to reveal anything that happened during the week or during the actual initiation ceremony. I didn't record any of it in my journal, but what transpired persists in my memory. Though it is sixty years later, I remain conflicted about how much of it to relate here. Most of what they put us through was illegal. But remember, no one told us hazing was outlawed. We were so totally imbued with the fraternity's cultural narrative we all believed it was simply the way things were done. And so it was.

Bits and pieces of information about what usually transpired during past Hell Weeks had been leaked, which helped us prepare for what was to come. The actives would use a combination of crude psychological manipulation and physical abuse to intimidate us. And it would work. I can still feel my sense of dread on the first night, afraid of what they would do to us.

A little after 10:00 p.m. on that Monday, led by Roosevelt "Rosie" Warren, who was the lead active for our probation, the six of us were ushered to the parking lot behind the Kappa House. Standing next to three cars were six more actives. Two of us were assigned to each car. Gerald rode with me. Rosie barked out orders—"Get in the cars and put these on!"—as each of us was given a blindfold. "Don't talk while we are driving," commanded our driver. For at least twenty minutes, the car made twists and turns so we couldn't determine the direction we were headed. Finally, the car stropped. "Keep your blindfolds on and get out!" bellowed Rosie.

Tradition held this was always the opening night formula. We knew where probates had been taken in the past, so we surmised we would be left at the same location, a few miles from the campus at Griffy Lake. Many of us had spent an evening with our girlfriends there. Each probate had hidden an extra dime on his person in case we were forced to empty our pockets of any change. A few days earlier, we scouted out the location of a phone booth to call a friend to bring us back to the campus.

It was a cold night for April. The crescent moon did little to penetrate the darkness. A slight breeze barely ruffled the leaves spring had recently delivered to the tree branches. From somewhere on the lake, we heard the mournful call of a loon, adding eeriness to the darkness. No one spoke. The six of us were lined up side by side. Rosie's voice shattered the silence: "Take off your blindfolds." We shivered not only from the low the temperature but because we were scared. It's difficult to express the sense of utter vulnerability and helplessness I felt at that moment.

The seven actives stood facing us. Not one was smiling. "All right, spread out and start running in place" was the next command, this time from Wayne McCoy. For the next half hour, they made us run around in the dark performing calisthenics and wind sprints. Then Rosie declared, "Now put your blindfolds back on and turn your backs to us. Do not move until we tell you to." After what seemed like an eternity, we heard the actives retreat to their cars and drive slowly away, stopping every few feet to see if we followed their directions. We remained still. When the sounds of their cars completely faded, we removed the blindfolds. After making sure everyone was accounted for, we agreed we were indeed at Griffy Lake. The pay phone located near the road leading into the lake was just a few minutes' walk from where they'd left us. It was well past midnight by the time we returned to the house. Of course, the whole event was really a charade because it always ended the same way; there was no mystery to how we would get back home.

A good deal of physical and psychological hazing occurred over the next three nights. We had to buy wooden paddles to carry with us wherever we went. They weren't simply ornamental. The actives used the paddles in a game called Kappa Ping Pong, with each of us as the ball. We were forced to eat all sorts of horrible stuff, including a live goldfish and a whole raw onion, dubbed a Kappa apple. On Friday, the legendary turn-back night, they put us through what the CIA could have used as an enhanced interrogation technique at one of its rendition sites. It was called crossing the Burning Sands, a phrase taken from the fraternity's initiation ritual, but this act had no resemblance to the one it described. I am not going to relate the specifics of what occurred, but for thirty minutes it was brutally painful. While we suffered, the actives kept singing their version of the old spiritual "Wade in the Water," changing the refrain to "This may be the last time" as they continued to administer the punishment. The thirty minutes seemed like thirty hours.

Surprisingly, in contradistinction to recent incidents of fraternity pledge abuse, alcohol was never involved in the Hell Week proceedings. Many of the Kappas drank at parties but rarely on their own in the house. While we did have occasional keggers, most often alcohol was consumed at a bar or at the Hole. Wild bouts of drinking were the province of the White frat boys. They even had a word for those sessions: a boress, pronounced "bore ass."

In any case, somehow, all of us successfully made it through the week, including crossing the Sands. In the early morning of April 14, 1962, we became full-fledged members of Kappa Alpha Psi Fraternity! Being kept awake all night left us exhausted but nonetheless exhilarated. The stone had been rolled away, and we had left the tomb; we were now big brothers! The question of what we, the newly minted actives, would do with the pledge class that followed didn't arise until much later.

In the meantime, we perceived this process to be a rite of passage based on tradition, not realizing tribal law had become liturgy. Very little of what transpired with us is part of the official initiation ritual. Today I view the entire experience as a combination of overreaching silliness and testosterone-fueled brutality. Without any doubt, all the hazing was totally wrong, but my understanding of that would only come later. Nevertheless, when it was over the joy and elation I experienced on that early Saturday morning are still fond memories. My journal entry that morning was a simple one: "Man, I am happy to be made!" My joy was compounded because Joan and I had continued seeing one another, and she was my date for the going-over dance that night.

A contingent of Kappas from one of our Chicago chapters drove to Bloomington for our going-over dance. This was my first chance as an active to meet brothers from another school. The Chicago brothers really enjoyed networking and partying with us that weekend. Before returning home, they invited all of the actives to come up to Chicago the next weekend for their chapter's going-over dance. Since that was our spring break, several of us decided to take them up on the invitation. A group of us drove up for the event. The trip included getting lost on the freeways going into and leaving the city. But in between there was a lot of serious partying.

Knowing what I know now, was it worth it? Would I do it again? Given the same set of circumstances, yes I would.

Returning to school as an active made the world appear much brighter. Unlike in high school, I not only had gained entry into the in group but had become a full-fledged member. Steve and I were once again on equal footing. The fraternity would not have another initiation until the fall, so soon the events of our Hell Week faded. Strangely, when we prepared for the next initiation and learned the details of the official fraternity initiation ritual, none of us appreciated the discrepancy between Kappa doctrine and what had happened to us. It is a prime example of how custom and peer pressure can overcome rational thought.

As I began to adjust to my new status, Freddie Stewart, along with Roosevelt Warren, began to mentor me in the ways of the fraternity and started grooming me to run for one of the chapter offices in May. Rosie, who I mentioned earlier, was a year ahead of me, also from Indianapolis, and was probably going to be elected the next chapter president, or polemarch. He was a capricious sort, outgoing and manly, but something in his manner made you question his sincerity. In spite of frequent exhibitions of false bravado, he usually didn't take himself too seriously and was able to laugh at his missteps. As a pledge I gave him a wide berth, so I didn't know him well. But after I was initiated, he showed what I thought was genuine interest in helping me to achieve a larger role in the frat. When the election was held, he became polemarch, and I was elected vice polemarch.

TWENTY-SIX

BE CAREFUL WHAT YOU ASK FOR

AT TIMES I SUFFERED from a nagging reluctance to ask an obvious question. In uncomfortable social situations, I often thought it better to avoid asking a probing question than to get a response I didn't want to hear. I didn't know what falling in love meant or felt like, but with Joan I thought I was there. "What do I do now?" I wondered. Trying to figure all this out led me to reexamine my situation. How to deal with this emotional conundrum was a mystery.

On an evening not long after the initiation dance, Joan and I had just returned arm in arm from the undergraduate library. Sitting in her dormitory lounge, we paid little attention to the few other couples scattered around the room. She looked lovely, and her mood matched her appearance. I decided this was the time to find out how she felt toward me.

As we snuggled close to each other on one of the lounge couches, I looked directly into her eyes and asked, "How do you feel about me?" Until that moment she had been wistful. Suddenly sitting up straight, surprised by my question, she became quiet and serious. She moved slightly away, and her countenance softened, then changed to a look of curiosity as she asked, "What do you mean?"

I repeated the question. She smiled compassionately as she responded, "I like you a great deal, but I'm not capable of liking anyone a real lot right now."

I should have stopped there, but I pressed further. "Do you ever think about me?"

Again she paused. "Yes." But then came her question. "Do you date other girls?"

"Not since I've been dating you."

"I think you should."

With Joan I had flipped my heart. I called heads; it landed on tails. Chastened but not defeated, I figured I still had one more chance. Earlier Joan had invited me to visit her in Fort Wayne for a weekend during the summer. I asked if the invitation still stood. She said it did if I wanted to come. I decided I would go.

As summer began to unfold, I made plans to drive the 125 miles from Indianapolis to Fort Wayne to see Joan. Despite the fact that we exchanged several letters and it was only a month away, time seemed as still as the humid air. I could barely wait to see her. As they say about best laid plans, mine abruptly changed.

I had never discussed my feelings for Joan with either of my parents, but they were well aware of them anyway. I had driven to Chicago a few months earlier with no complaint from them. I simply announced my plans the day before I planned to leave. My mom and dad were in the kitchen that Friday evening. "By the way, I'm driving up to Fort Wayne tomorrow to spend a weekend with Joan at her parents' home."

My dad exploded! His jaw stiffened. He pulled himself up to his full height and told me, "You're not going." He then turned and walked out of the kitchen.

My mother's face was a picture of surprise and dismay, but she remained silent. I was blindsided and dumbfounded by his declaration. "What?" I responded angrily as I followed him out of the kitchen. This only increased his anger at my audacity to resist him.

"You're not going!" he said again, only with much more force as he turned and faced me.

"I'm nineteen years old, and I can make my own decisions. I'm going!"

"If you do, I will see you transfer to DePauw (University), where there aren't many colored girls, and I'll tell L.L. to stop paying your expenses!"

We were about to come to blows after those threats. Despite being enraged, I knew I had too much to lose by pressing my case any further. He was not bluffing; this was a battle I could only lose. Without further resistance, I turned away and left the house. When I returned three hours later, I found my mother had intervened. By then my father had gone to bed. My mother and I sat in our living room, which was not our usual spot for a conversation, and she quietly began to explain.

"It took a while for your father to calm down. After I fixed dinner, I said, 'Cal, why are you so upset about Lester going to see his girlfriend?'"

"He's going to drive up there and get married," my father had said. "That will ruin him."

"Get married?" Mom replied. "He's not getting married. He's planning to be a doctor. He knows what would happen if he got that serious with Joan. He just wants to see her."

She added that they'd had a more lengthy conversation, but that was the gist of it. At the end she reassured him that marrying Joan was not in the cards. My dad was a person who found it difficult to admit he was wrong and to apologize. This episode underscored his fear I would deviate from the path he planned for me, causing his dreams to come crashing down. The following morning he told me I could go after all, but it was too late. I had already called Joan to tell her I wasn't coming, making up an excuse because my fragile ego would not permit me to disclose the real reason. We agreed I would drive up the following weekend.

Upon my arrival in Fort Wayne, I was greeted like a member of the family, and I overheard Joan's mother referring to me as her "boyfriend." I spent the entire weekend with Joan. Both of us seemed to enjoy the time together. After I returned home, we exchanged a few letters over the remainder of the summer, but I had to recognize what I already intuitively knew: my effort to win her would be a failure.

Many years later, in 1997, I was in New York City and had dinner with a mutual friend Sandy Brown and her husband. I asked if she was still in contact with Joan. I knew they had been good friends. She said yes, then told me Joan had completed her undergraduate studies at Howard University, married an ophthalmologist, had two children, and settled in Dallas. The following day, I received a call from Sandy. She had spoken with Joan and learned she was in town visiting her daughter.

"I told her you were in the city," Sandy said. "She would like to talk with you."

It had been more than thirty years since we'd last seen each other. When I called her, we reminisced for a few minutes, then I reminded her how hard I had tried to win her affection back at IU, and how I almost literally worshiped the ground she walked on. When I finished, there was a slight pause, then she said, "Oh, really?"

Surprised, I exclaimed, "I've been pining away for you for thirty years, and you don't even remember?"

She responded, "Of course I do."

We both laughed.

TWENTY-SEVEN

WELCOME TO THE WORLD OF
THE BLACK WORKING CLASS

WITH MY FIRST YEAR of college completed, I was back at home looking for a summer job. My spot at the supermarket was no longer available. In the past I had used my father's connections, but now I was trying on my own. It was almost June, and I had no success!

However, two days before the start of the Memorial Day weekend, something came through. I was offered a job as a janitor at the Eli Lilly pharmaceutical plant located on the South Side of Indianapolis. The company is still one of the city's major employers. The chairman of the board's granddaughter was a high school acquaintance, but she had nothing to do with me getting the job. It was just one of the many places I applied. It was a menial job, but one of the few available to Blacks at the company. Though I considered it "Toming," as in being an Uncle Tom, I needed a job. I sat on my ego and was okay with it. The salary was $73 per week. Working at the supermarket had taught me how to perform the basics of janitorial work. Since I was a college kid as well as the youngest employee in the department, I planned to work hard to avoid displaying any hint of condescension and to make a good impression.

The Eli Lilly complex is a huge collection of buildings located in a mixed industrial and lower socioeconomic residential neighborhood south of the downtown core, then referred to as the South Side. As you approached the plant, the air was often filled with a pungent odor emanating from somewhere within it. I remember thinking how bad it would be to live nearby.

Day one began in the employment office. After filling out the requisite paperwork, I was taken to the service department to meet the man in charge. He was a balding, portly, very dark-skinned Black man who usually had the stub of an unlit cigar either in an ashtray on his desk or in one corner of his mouth. I don't remember his name, but his staff referred to him as the Chief or just Chief. I was the only college-age male summer replacement worker in the department. There were also one or two White coeds assigned to the cafeteria.

The Chief explained my duties. The job involved mopping; kitchen work, consisting of busing tables and dishwashing; and a lot of dusting, sweeping, and window washing. I would fill in for one of the regulars during vacations and perform tasks that were scheduled to be done only during the summer months. Getting to know the men in the department gave me an intimate view of the effects of entrenched racism in the workplace in Indianapolis, reinforcing how necessary it was to obtain a college education. There were seven or eight men in the department. I guessed their ages ranged from early thirties to early fifties. When I arrived, they greeted me cordially. It didn't require much time to learn the pecking order in the group or to accept my place at the bottom of it. I made a great effort to fit in with these older guys. Initially, the men kidded me, but it was good-natured; each of them was always willing to help if I needed it.

I witnessed an interesting dynamic at play between the Chief and his staff. Whenever he was present they were deferential, but it was strictly a facade, similar to how I imagine field slaves behaved in the presence of the highest-ranking house slave, sometimes referred to as the driver. Their solicitousness was insincere; they mocked him as an Uncle Tom when he was not around because they felt he constantly kowtowed to his White superiors. Each morning we'd arrive in the locker room, change into our work uniforms, clock in, then meet the Chief at his office to learn our assignments.

Three of my former workmates stand out in my memory. James, who was brash, upbeat, and probably in his late forties, was particularly notable. Short and stocky, with an air of street smartness, he was a classic trash talker. There was a pool table in the lounge. Often, he and I would shoot a game of eight ball. He beat me twelve times in a row! To make matters worse, as he was beating me he talked smack, but it was always light hearted—for example, "You know, young dude, you are really a turkey!" The last game we played was on my final day at the job. By then all the other guys knew the game tally and paid attention. I won, bringing cheers all around, even from James.

Nick was probably in his early fifties and had worked at the same job for twenty-plus years. He had done sufficiently well that he owned a small dry cleaner's near my old neighborhood. Though Nick was pleasant and generally soft spoken, there was an aspect of his personality suggesting he had also done his time on the streets and had grown past it. He was always the first person to offer me a hand and the man I came to know best. One of his physical characteristics intrigued me. He had undergone a surgical procedure that interrupted the right chain of his sympathetic nervous system; the result prevented him from perspiring on that side. It was really odd to witness his left side saturated with sweat and the opposite side bone dry!

Last, there was Gregory, who was probably in his late thirties. He was short, handsome, fair-skinned, and freckled, with piercing grey eyes. His manner suggested he had been a player in his youth, which may have been why he was divorced with three kids. When I remarked about the unusual color of his eyes, he related this story: He had been in the army, and while he was stationed in Germany, a woman he was seeing described his eyes as *Katzenaugen*, which means cat's eyes. I suspected she had other more intimate German descriptions of him he didn't choose to share with me. No matter. He was really an engaging guy to be around. One day at lunch he began talking about his past. With a resigned expression as he spoke, he described failing to finish school as one of his biggest regrets because other events in his life had gotten him sidetracked. I thought he was referring to college; he meant high school! None of the men in the department had progressed beyond the twelfth grade. My first experience working with a group of Black men was revealing. Witnessing how their aspirations had been quashed by racism was disheartening and an eye opener.

FIGURE 1. Mr. Goodman's home on Kessler Boulevard.

FIGURE 2.   My baby picture, 1943.

FIGURE 3. Mom and Dad with me, age four, in front of Bethel AME Church.

ABOVE, FIGURE 4. At age six on my grandparents' tobacco farm in Kentucky, sitting in my grandfather's wagon pulled by his two mules.

FACING, FIGURE 5. At age eight in my Cub Scout uniform in front of our apartment building.

FIGURE 6. My seventh grade class picture.

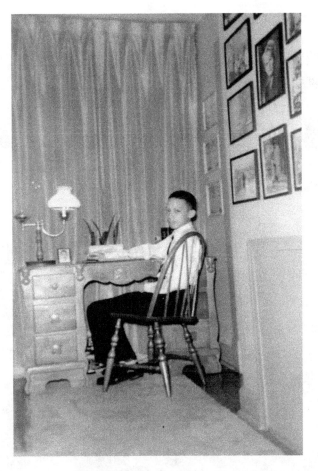

FIGURE 7. At my desk in my family's apartment; I was about twelve.

FIGURE 8. At age thirteen standing outside Smithwood Dormitory on my first trip to the IU campus in Bloomington.

FIGURE 9. Dad in his barbershop in the Illinois Building in downtown Indianapolis.

FIGURE 10. At age fifteen with Nancy Streets, the first African American Miss Indiana University.

FIGURE 11. Our home on West Thirty-Seventh Street.

FIGURE 12. Mr. Goodman, my dad, and me, age sixteen, in Mr. Goodman's new home.

FIGURE 13. Mr. Goodman's daughter, Sue, with me at his home.

FIGURE 14. Jason, my first college roommate, with me.

FIGURE 15. The brand-new Kappa Alpha Psi fraternity house on IU's campus in Bloomington, 1962.

FIGURE 16. Joan Stanton outside the library in the spring of 1962.

FIGURE 17. The morning of our initiation, when the six of us had just become actives, April 1962.

FIGURE 18. Singing the song we composed at our initiation dance later that night.

FIGURE 19. Harold and Steve with me, in the living room of the Kappa house.

FIGURE 20. The first time I sang "Zum Gali" in public at one of our initiation dances, fall 1963.

FIGURE 21. With Gloria Francis, fall 1963.

FIGURE 22. My third year of medical school.

FIGURE 23. With Dean Irwin and my dad at my medical school graduation, 1968.

Year Two

1962–1963

TWENTY-EIGHT

LICKETY-SPLIT

THE SUMMER OF 1962 quickly evaporated, and soon I was back on campus. I had not been able to move my GPA to my first semester midterm grade of 3.0; it hovered around 2.6 Though Mr. Goodman didn't make any comment to me about my grades, I knew my parents expected more, and most likely he did as well. Further emphasis on my studies was required—more work and less play. So when I returned to Bloomington to begin my second year, I knew what I had to do to improve my grades. I had several tough courses ahead.

Joan returned to IU for the fall semester. We remained friends and even shared some moments of intimacy, but I finally accepted reality. She left Bloomington at the end of the fall semester.

Organic chemistry lecture and lab were required prerequisites. Organic would be my most challenging academic subject of the entire year. Having achieved an A in freshman chemistry, I felt pretty good about how I would be able to handle this course. The class stands out in my memory not so much because of its difficulty, though there was that, but because of my instructor. His name is lost to me, but I remember him because of his appearance and some of his peculiar habits and mannerisms. He followed a consistent routine when he lectured. Arriving several minutes before the beginning of the class, he would fill the two blackboards with notes. When he finished, two or three minutes typically remained before the bell rang to begin. Generally, he would lean forward, arms straight, with his hands resting against the lab table next to the lectern, and without saying a word he would just stare into the room.

Though he was a PhD and wore a suit (usually blue) and tie, I thought he looked more like a farmer than a college professor. He was tall and stocky, with a slightly stooped posture and a weathered face and hands. As soon as the bell rang, bam, it was off to the races! He began speaking rapidly and did not stop until the bell sounded again, indicating the end of the period. He spoke so quickly, we could barely take notes. We also learned fast that unless we arrived early, there was no time to copy what he had written on the blackboards and then take notes during the lecture. So we did arrive early, and we compared our lecture notes after class to see if we had missed anything. It was a tough subject for me and more of a struggle than I anticipated, but I finished with a final grade of B.

TWENTY-NINE

ARMAGEDDON?

AS WE WENT ABOUT our daily routines, the gravity of a momentous global event shattered our complacency. Between the sixteenth and twenty-eighth of October 1962, the United States and the Soviet Union barely avoided going to war. Those were the dates of the Cuban Missile Crisis.

We followed the news and knew about the presence of Russian ballistic missiles in Cuba, but we weren't prepared for what happened next. President Kennedy wanted the missiles removed, and the Russians refused. Khrushchev and Kennedy then called each other's bluff and were engaged in what was essentially a global Cold War game of chicken. Russian naval vessels headed to the Caribbean to breach the US Navy's blockade of the island.

I clearly recall the anxiety and outright fear that gripped the nation as the Russian ships moved closer and closer. We were totally engrossed by it. On what turned out to be the final day of the crisis, we were glued to our TVs and radios, afraid that World War III was about to commence. Nothing else seemed to matter as we waited for Armageddon. I still remember the dread we experienced until Kennedy and Khrushchev reached a last-minute compromise that averted the crisis.

It was the first time I can recall when the nation was traumatized by an existential event. It would not be the last during my time in Bloomington.

THIRTY

THE UNANTICIPATED PRICE
OF BROTHERHOOD

HAVING BEEN INITIATED THE previous April and then elected vice polemarch in May, I knew school and the fraternity would be plenty to keep me busy during my sophomore year. Rosie's efforts to increase my involvement in fraternity affairs seemed to work. The big issues on the frat's agenda, in addition to the day-to-day management of the house, were recruiting a new pledge class, which we hoped would allow us to fill it to capacity, improving the fraternity's GPA, and deciding on a date for the next probation and going-over dance. I was marginally involved in chapter finances, and I learned they were strained.

At one point, Rosie shared with me the news that no funds for house maintenance were coming from the Grand Chapter. I was shocked and replied, "That's crazy! No wonder the chapter has problems paying the bills on time! How did that happen?'" Rosie didn't have an answer. Our financial condition failed to improve after our smoker, mainly because the house remained only half full. Making matters worse, several of the occupants were late in paying their housing assessments, putting further strain on our finances.

A November date for probation and the initiation dance was set. It would be my first as an active. I had little input into the planning; Rosie and some of the other actives dealt with those issues. It was no surprise my perspective was very different from a few months earlier, when I was a probate. I felt neither compassion nor empathy for these probates, only the powerful satisfaction of moving from a subordinate to a superior status. The path leading from being abused to becoming an abuser was unknown to me. I assumed the process was just what we believed it to be: a rite of passage. I had no idea the code of "if I went through it, now you have to" was in reality the fusion of hierarchal power dynamics and tribal law. It was simply the subjugation of one group by another, a microcosmic reflection of Jim Crow racism in American society at large.

The six days of Hell Week were a replay of my own experience, differing only with me being on the other side. Toward the end of the week, I did begin to empathize with the pledges' struggles but failed to acknowledge this whole process was ridiculous barbarism. Turn-back night and crossing the Sands were just as brutal as they had been with my fellow Scrollers and me six month earlier. By early Saturday morning, the initiation ritual was complete. We brought five new brothers into the fold, and all was once again well. All sins were forgiven.

The veneer of brotherhood began to peel away a few days later. Things were not going well between the actives and the current pledge class. In an attempt to reconcile the situation, the Scrollers requested a meeting with the actives to air their grievances. Rosie's haughty attitude was one of their complaints. His arrogance was degrading; they resented it. Before scheduling the meeting, several of us caught wind of the pledges' primary complaint. We corralled Rosie and told him to back off, to drop the attitude, and to stop acting so shitty. Though he may have been unconvinced, he agreed. So the meeting was avoided. This pacified the pledges for a time. It was my first awareness of smoldering tensions between the Scrollers and us actives. There would be more flare-ups.

The axiom "boys will be boys" was alive and well. There were frivolous moments as well as more serous ones. One time we had a shaving cream fight. I don't remember how it began, but it ended with most of us chasing each other through the second-floor hallways with spray cans of shaving cream. In the end, shaving cream covered almost everything and everybody, but we laughed as we cleaned it up.

THIRTY-ONE

LIFE AS AN ACTIVE BECOMES REAL

THE ANNUAL NATIONAL CONVENTION of the fraternity, the Grand Conclave, was to be held in Toledo, Ohio, during Christmas break of my sophomore year. Rosie was a delegate, so the day after Christmas he, along with several of us, decided to make the four-and-a-half hour drive to attend. It would be my first convention, so I was excitedly anticipating the trip.

Coincident with the sessions, there was a schedule of social events for the undergraduates. The first of these was a Meet Your Date mixer set for Thursday evening, the day before the opening session. We knew practically nothing about Toledo, so what kind of city we would encounter was a mystery when we arrived early Thursday afternoon. Before checking into our hotel, we wanted to grab something to eat. Our intention was to locate a restaurant where we could get a down-home meal, which meant finding one in a Black neighborhood. But none of us knew where to look. An attempt to find one by just driving around the city was unsuccessful.

While we were stopped at a traffic light, a police squad car pulled up next to the driver's side of our car. Gilbert, the driver, motioned for the policeman riding in the passenger seat to roll down his window, then he asked the two White cops, "Where do all the colored people live in this town?"

The officer in the passenger seat looked a little embarrassed. After a pause he replied, "They're all over."

Gilbert continued, "We're from out of town and are looking for a place to eat."

At that the officer turned to his partner, then looked back at Gilbert, smiled sheepishly, and gave us directions to a restaurant located in what seemed to be the heart of a Black neighborhood. When we arrived at the address, it looked more like a storefront than a restaurant. It was only late afternoon, but there was no one on the street, and it appeared to be closed. However, when we approached the building, the door was slightly ajar, so we peered inside; the seating area was dark, but we saw a light in the back possibly coming from the kitchen.

Rosie asked, "Is there anyone here?"

A stern-looking older Black woman, resembling one of our grandmothers, appeared, wiping her hands on her apron as she walked from the kitchen. "What do you want? We aren't open yet."

We explained who we were and why we were there.

Her face softened as she smiled then said, "Why, you boys come on in sit down, and I'll fix you something to eat."

It was a delicious down-home meal, with fried chicken, mashed potatoes, greens, and cornbread, topped off with warm peach cobbler. Even now, I'm struck by the fact that two White policemen directed us to that restaurant and the warmth we experienced from the woman who served us, making us feel right at home. I seriously doubt in 1962 we would have been treated as well in a similar situation in a White neighborhood.

Once we checked into our hotel, the next order of business should have been getting registered for the meeting and deciding which sessions we planned to attend. But since only Rosie was a delegate, the rest of us got ready for the mixer, with the goal of securing dates for the dance that night and, hopefully, for the entire weekend.

When we arrived at the mixer, the large room was filled with college kids from all over the country. Initially, there wasn't much mixing. The out-of-town brothers chiefly stood around eyeing the women in the room. The women appeared to be scrutinizing the men as well, waiting for one of them to make a move.

One of the hosts introduced two of us to Effie Slaughter, who was featured in the lead article regarding this meeting in the *Kappa Journal*. She later became the wife of Marion Barry, the controversial two-time mayor of Washington, DC. Effie was stunningly attractive and accordingly drew a lot of attention. Guys swarmed to her like drones around a queen bee. I felt she was out of my league. After two unsuccessful tries, I got a date—Carolyn—for Thursday night. Before we parted, she accepted my offer to see her again the following night.

After spending Friday at the convention, which I found exceedingly boring, that evening things went south. Carolyn stood me up. Our culture required manhood be earned, but once achieved the mantle was precarious and could be easily lost. Set adrift once again, I must have looked lost when a brother from Toledo, whom I'd met the day before, told me he knew of another dance and suggested we go check it out. By sheer luck I met the girl I wished I had met on the first night: Mary Goodwin. Despite the evening's tenuous beginnings, meeting Mary salvaged the entire trip and helped repair my wounded ego.

With the start of the spring semester, I seemed to be gaining status as a leader in the chapter. No matter my elevated status, I was not beyond criticism. I shouldn't have been so naive to think I would be immune to it. One night, after we had retired to our beds in the second floor dorm, three of our pledges—Willie (Townes), Willie (Turner), and Randy Phillips—stayed awake and talked. It was impossible to ignore them. Their conversation covered almost everybody on campus's business, including mine.

Townes: "Even with that car, he still ain't shit!"

Turner: "He's dating Jodie Bell."

Townes: "You mean he'd like to. She dates the car, and he's driving it. He's got too many exams. If you want something like that, you got to put some time into it. His game is too weak."

I was not bothered by their opinions because from my vantage point, things were going well. But another unanticipated criticism gave me pause, leading to some self-reflection. At dinner one evening, Rosie and "Duddy" Gales (another active) told me I was stingy.

"You made us pay you to catch a ride back to the campus from Naptown [a common name for Indianapolis before it became Indy]," Rosie complained.

"My father would never charge anyone for simply riding along," added Duddy.

Their complaint stemmed from the two dollars I had charged each of them to bring them with me back to Bloomington. A bus ticket cost about the same amount. I countered by saying, "My mother advised me to charge you." I never thought to question her advice until they raised it as an issue. Being an only child, I wasn't expert at sharing. I decided they were right and never charged anyone again for riding along.

THIRTY-TWO

THE ELUSIVE 3.0 GPA

AT THE BEGINNING OF the spring semester, my social life, academics, and the fraternity met head on. Joan had left, I wasn't making the degree of progress I hoped with the girl I was dating, I had still only achieved only a 2.5 GPA, and there were more difficult courses ahead. Mr. Goodman didn't register any comment about my grades, but my parents expressed concern. Some of my close friends failed to make their grades and flunked out. Quite a few of the pledges also failed to achieve a C grade average, so the frat's marginal GPA was a serious problem. It was apparent we needed to place an even greater emphasis on academic achievement when deciding on potential candidates for the next Scroller class.

Developmental Vertebrate Anatomy was my most important course in the spring of 1963. Our instructor, "Terrible Ted" Torrey, had all the qualities of a zombie. He appeared ancient and spoke with a profound lisp in a soft, almost haunting voice. Years earlier, one of my classmates' dads had been one of his pupils. When Dr. Torrey was returning a set of test papers, he stopped at my friend's desk and remarked, "Your dad got an A."

A month into the semester, Dr. Torrey introduced a surprise guest lecturer, Dr. James Watson. An IU alumnus, he spoke about the new molecule he and his colleagues had discovered a few years earlier. They had been awarded the Nobel Prize in Physiology the previous year for the discovery of DNA. Though we had no idea about the significance of their discovery, receiving a lecture from a Nobel laureate was really exciting.

THIRTY-THREE

HERE COME THE SAMMIES

AS I NOTED EARLIER, there was no overt animosity between our fraternity and the White fraternities; still, our social relationships were limited to the Jewish Greeks. Doug Barton, one of the Sigma Alpha Mu (the Sammies) actives, was a friend of mine. Pete, his pledge son, called me to ask a favor. Their pledge class was embroiled in a conflict with the actives. Consequently, they scheduled a surprise walkout for the next day, planning to travel by bus to Miami University of Ohio for the weekend. They wanted to store their luggage at our house the night before they left then retrieve it on their way to board the bus. I agreed.

I thought we Kappas were uninhibited, but our pranks paled in comparison to some of the antics pulled by the White and Jewish frats. Strangely, when conflicts arose between their actives and pledges, frequently the pledges took out their anger by trashing the house, then disappearing before being apprehended. We found that type of self-destructive behavior strange. Why would you want to vandalize your own house?

Anyway, on this occasion, before escaping, the Sammie pledges ransacked their house. For example, they removed the water faucets and put one of their actives' VW Bug in the dining hall along with a host of other crazy pranks. They rendezvoused at our house before rushing to the bus they'd chartered. Two of them wouldn't have made it on their own, so I drove them to the bus, arriving just as some of the angry actives were coming after them. I suspected there would be hell to pay when they returned. Later, I learned the pledges' parents just paid whatever fines were levied by the actives.

A couple of weeks later, the Sammies held a dance at their house and we were invited. Three of us dropped by with our dates. The next characterization will sound too stereotypical and a bit racist, but it's accurate. It was a widely held belief among us African American students that none of the White kids had any clue how to dance. For us, dancing meant performing a specific, named dance such as the Boogaloo or the Philly Dog. One did not just dance. In contrast, it appeared to us when the White kids danced all they did was jump up and down, flailing their arms about. They seemed awed by our dance steps, and we loved to show off! Our appearance at the Sammie gig was no exception. The party livened up after we arrived.

Speaking of the Sammies, one of the more memorable characters I met at IU was a Sammie pledge from East Chicago, Irving "Irv" Goodman (no relation to L.L. Goodman). Let me take a moment to explain why he was unique. Though brought up in a traditional, conservative Jewish household, Irv was, paradoxically, a very free spirit. He had gone to a predominantly Black high school and had become saturated with the culture, particularly the language. For example, if you saw him on campus and greeted him with "Hi, Irv!" he would typically respond, "What's happenin', Papa?" He wasn't trying to sound Black; it's just the way he spoke.

One semester Irv and I were part of a carpool to the main campus for eight o'clock classes (the Sammie house was located near ours). As you can imagine, most of us were still half asleep, and no one was interested in engaging in spirited conversation along the way. One particular day, we were headed down Jordan Avenue when Irv decided to talk to God—out loud.

"Good morning, God! Isn't this a beautiful day? How are you doing up there?"

Not surprisingly, this did not go over well with the rest us. Someone said, "Shut up, Irv! God's not awake yet. And if he was, he wouldn't want to talk to you!"

But that was simply Irv being himself.

He and I became good friends. Though we kept in contact after we left IU, I saw him only once more. It was 1969 in La Jolla, California. Having just entered the US Navy, I was temporarily stationed nearby at Camp Pendleton.

I knew Irv lived in the area, so I called him to see if we could meet. He was his usual self when we spoke, and he asked where I was calling from.

"I'm standing in the lobby of newly opened Holiday Inn in La Jolla," I replied. "This was the closest spot where I thought I could locate a pay phone."

"Give me the address and I'll be there in twenty minutes."

A short while later, Irv walked through the door, arms wide open, with a big smile. "What's happenin', Papa?"

He had graduated from law school and was in the midst of studying for the state bar exam. Following a brief "what have you been up to" conversation, he suggested we head to one of his favorite spots to grab a burger and a beer. After conversing for most of the evening, I needed to head back to the base. Before parting, we vowed to keep in touch. Sadly, we lost contact not long after. Last year, a mutual friend and classmate told me Irv had passed away several years earlier.

THIRTY-FOUR

JOY AND SORROW INTERLACED

ONE OF OUR MOST fun social events was a mock casino night at the house for our dates and ourselves. The money was fake, but once everyone started gambling, you would have thought the cash was real. One of the football players, Willie Townes, fancied himself somewhat of a card shark. He devised a game he called "find the red card hidden in the deck." After a while, the red card had been picked so often it was essentially marked, but he continued playing the game anyway. At one point he bet $3,800 no one could locate the card. He lost. Despite his lack of gaming prowess, Willie went on to play professional football for three NFL teams, including the Dallas Cowboys.

I never thought of myself as a confidant, but some in the frat apparently felt otherwise. Perhaps it was a reflection of the respect I had achieved as vice polemarch. One evening, I was reading a textbook. Mike Snorden, one of the Scrollers, appeared outside my open study room door and asked, "May I come in and talk with you?"

"Sure," I replied. "What about?"

His mother had suffered a spinal cord injury from a fall down a flight of stairs, rendering her a quadriplegic. Initially she wasn't expected to live, but she survived and was determined she would be able to walk again, though her doctors disagreed. Mike was terribly distressed and worried about her. I didn't ask why he chose to seek me out for counsel, but I wanted to help him as best I could.

Recalling my struggle to offer Elsie's parents words of comfort after her death, I hoped I could find a way to offer some measure of support to Mike. I tried to recall a biblical verse that might provide solace but couldn't think of one I thought appropriate. One of my favorite books of prose and poetry was *The Prophet*, by Kahlil Gibran. In it, the author relates the story of a prophet speaking to his followers about a variety of topics. I highlighted one chapter, "On Pain," and offered Mike my copy to read. About fifteen minutes later, I heard another knock at my door. It was Mike. He had read the passage and wanted me to know he was grateful. I did not see him again after we finished college, but I recently learned he developed COVID-19 and passed away. In another attempt to provide solace, this time to his family, I sent my condolences.

THIRTY-FIVE

THE HORN SOUNDED AND THE WALLS CAME TUMBLING DOWN

DESPITE LIP SERVICE TO cohesiveness and brotherhood, smoldering tensions between the pledges and actives and friction between some of the older actives and us younger ones rose to the surface yet again.

Rosie was again acting capriciously with the Scrollers. Without consulting any of us, one Sunday afternoon he posted a notice on the bulletin board stating he was holding a "symposium" in the library at 11:15 p.m. for all the pledges and any actives who wanted to attend. There was no indication why he called the meeting or his agenda.

Most of the brothers, including me, chuckled at the idea and ignored it. But when the time for the meeting arrived, Rosie asked me to sit in with him. I agreed. However, when no one else appeared at the appointed time, I retreated into the TV room, leaving Rosie alone in the library. Twenty minutes later, I returned to see if the meeting was underway. Peering through the glass door, I saw him and some of the pledges in the midst of a discussion. A few minutes after that, several other actives arrived, and we went in together.

The moment I entered the library, I sensed something was seriously wrong. A storm was brewing. The pledges seemed tense. Rosie appeared to be needling them; he was annoyed that some were missing and that those present had arrived late. When we entered the library, Rosie paused the discussion to wait for the rest of the pledges to arrive. We quietly seated ourselves. A short while later, at my request, Ronnie, the pledge dean, entered the library. Finally, the rest of the pledges finally appeared.

Rosie brought the meeting to order. He asked me to take minutes. Starting with the actives, I surveyed the room trying to gauge by their body language what they might be thinking. Tom sat quietly in a chair by the desk. My chair was in front of the desk. Freddie was on the floor beside me. Ronnie remained standing. The probates looked sleepy and anxious. Scrutinizing the rest of the pledges, I noted some looked bored, a few appeared indifferent, and one or two others looked worried. It was not yet clear why Rosie had called the meeting. He began by opening the floor to the pledges to express their griev-ances. As each one did, the rest of us remained silent. Tension in the room continued to mount.

A few minutes later, Gerald Adams and Kenny Ellis, two more actives, joined the group. Gerald suddenly interrupted the discussion to make a state-ment. It was a complaint against Rosie! Surprised, Rosie asked him to wait until the pledges were finished, and he agreed. When his turn came, Gerald started on Rosie anew. He began by complaining about the meeting time, followed by detailing several personal issues he had with Rosie. Shortly after Gerald finished, Rosie ended the meeting with no action planned or taken on any of the issues raised. The pledges left, Gerald with them. Rosie asked the rest of us to remain for a moment.

"I waited until the Scrollers left to say something, but I wish Gerald were here to hear it," he said. He continued, stating he believed Gerald was totally wrong to voice his complaints by interrupting the ongoing discussion. There was general agreement it was inappropriate for Gerald to unload his personal grievances against Rosie with the pledges present. All the while Kenny, now the only one in the room standing, paced back and forth, angrily snapping a necktie against the furniture. Because of his football player physique (six feet, two inches tall and over two hundred pounds), coupled with being seriously pissed off, he was an intimidating figure.

We began to discuss what issues the pledges might have had with the way they were being treated by us actives. Some of us thought, based on tradition, things were as they should be. Others, including Gerald, who had returned, disagreed. The discussion devolved into arguments between the old school and us more recently minted actives, and it became personal. The disagree-ments continued for another hour, ending with no resolution to any of the issues but leaving some hard feelings behind, particularly between Gerald and

Kenny. The old schoolers wanted Lobo's input, since he was one of them, but he was not at the meeting.

With the exception of Freddie, Lobo was the oldest active. For a variety of reasons, he was already a fabled character at Alpha chapter. Lobo's given name was Charles Taylor, but no one called him that; it was always just Lobo. Without a doubt, he was the first person I came to know who had literally become a legend in his own time.

Lobo grew up in Gary, Indiana, and entered IU in the mid-1950s. He graduated ten years later. One could write a book dedicated to his story, but that's not my intention. Nonetheless, Lobo weaved in and out of my life during my time on campus. He was a sizable figure, also over six feet tall with a muscular physique like Kenny, but slightly shorter and heavier. He was blessed or cursed (it varied depending on whom you asked) with a silver tongue and a persuasive manner that made him one of the best con artists I've encountered and the first one I came to know well. He also had a darker and more sinister side that made his nickname all the more fitting. The primary reason Lobo remained in Bloomington for all those years was because of an unpaid debt to the university. It seems as he was approaching the end of his final semester and could no longer finesse not paying the debt, he wasn't allowed to graduate. In 1964, he finally retired the debt.

There seemed to be few boundaries around what Lobo would do to survive. Most often, he would mooch as much as he could from his friends inside and outside the fraternity until they finally cut him off. Then he would go into Bloomington and usually find a decent job. For example, he often worked in construction. After six months or so, he would have saved enough money to stop working and support himself for a while, again often aided by his friends. When his funds and his friends' patience ran out, he would repeat the cycle. You couldn't help but admire his resourcefulness. He spent a lot of his free time around the Kappa house, though he was inactive. Lobo happened to be away from the campus the evening of the Sunday meeting. We tacitly agreed to let things simmer until he came back.

Upon his return, Lobo was briefed on the aforementioned meeting and asked to offer his thoughts on how we could resolve the growing divide between the Scrollers and ourselves, as well as the gulf between the two groups of actives. His advice was simple: remember we were once pledges, listen to their complaints, and treat them fairly. About our flagging brotherhood, he said the only thing that mattered was once we shook hands as brothers, brothers we were for better or worse. Oddly, his words were enough to calm the waters for a while.

THIRTY-SIX

SECOND VERSE, SAME AS THE FIRST?

IT WAS TIME TO take the next group of Scrollers through another probation. Although fewer than six months had elapsed since I enthusiastically participated in my first probation as an active, this time it was different. The fun was gone. Only because it was required did I feel the need to participate at all. Not understanding why, I knew that something within me had altered my perspective. Perhaps at some unconscious level I recognized this ritual was brutal and unnecessary, or possibly I was simply distressed over the amount of my time required to participate. I'm still uncertain.

On the third night, Hell Week reached a new low. Kenny slapped Mike Snorden, one of the probates, which almost precipitated a fight. Mike was about as well put together as Kenny, so serious injuries could have resulted if they had gotten into it. At the last moment, Freddie rushed in to intervene and stop the conflict from escalating further. He ushered the probates out of the house for the remainder of the night. When Kenny offered no sign of contrition, Freddie reproached him about his behavior, causing Kenny's anger to increase, but now it was directed toward Freddie. Though they avoided coming to blows, I don't believe they spoke to each other for the remainder of the night or the next day.

The following night, at song practice, the atmosphere remained tense. The animosity between Kenny and Freddie had not subsided. Kenny kept needling him until he finally had enough and exploded. Despite Kenny being much larger, for a second time they almost came to blows. Picture a struggle between a bear and a wolverine. When Gerald came to Freddie's defense, Kenny turned his ire toward him. To make matters worse, because the upcoming dance was cosponsored by the AKAs, several of them were present to witness all the turmoil. Our dirty laundry was on full display.

What role did I play in this scene? None! I wasn't in charge and had no clue how to defuse the conflict. By sheer happenstance, Albert Spurlock, one of the high-ranking Grand Chapter officials who lived in Indianapolis, decided to make an unannounced visit to the campus to check on us. He was the coach of one of the city's top men's high school basketball teams. He walked into the middle of this tumult. I did not record any details regarding how he managed it, but taking them aside, he facilitated a dialogue between the warring parties and defused the situation. I wrote only one comment about what occurred: "We talked it out." Witnessing this de-escalation was an important lesson in conflict resolution. Afterward, there was no further talk of the conflict. We were able to finish the song practice.

The remainder of the week passed without further blowups. By week's end, the probates had become brothers, and once more old conflicts and grievances were put aside.

In contrast to the tumultuous events of the preceding week, the dance on Saturday night produced one of my most unforgettable moments. I was tabbed to sing lead on our rendition of "Zum Gali." It's an adaptation of an Israeli children's folk song often sung by the Kappas at going-over dances. In our version, the melody remains the same, but it's sung more slowly with custom lyrics. No one outside the frat knew I had a pretty good tenor voice. When I stepped out in front at the dance, I knew it would be a surprise—and indeed it was. As I began my solo, I heard screams from some of the women in the ballroom; a few of them literally ran up to the line and sat on the floor in front of me. Talk about an ego trip! I thought this must be how Elvis felt when he took the stage.

THIRTY-SEVEN

WITH POWER COMES RESPONSIBILITY

THE SPRING SEMESTER WOUND routinely toward its conclusion until it reached May, the time to elect chapter officers for the next school year. Along with Ronnie Finnell, I was nominated to be our next polemarch. Torn between wanting the position because of its prestige and the measure of faith placed in me by the brothers and my uncertainty in being able to handle the office, I was conflicted over my candidacy.

Though Ronnie and I had graduated from the same high school and had been initiated in the same group, he was two years older and a whole lot cooler. In my view, he had achieved a greater level of respect than I. Given the condition of fraternity affairs, neither of us aggressively sought the office. The chapter's internecine conflicts, marginal GPA, and precarious finances frustrated us both. Finally, Ronnie had enough and bowed out of the race. Though he withdrew, his name remained on the ballot. No other candidate stepped up at the last moment. I won by a big margin, merely by default. In the end, it didn't matter. I would be at the helm, and I had to plot a course to try to rescue Alpha chapter.

As the conflicts continued, I searched for strategies to deal with them. One of the first problems I encountered was a questionable grade for one of the pledges, Willie Turner. The previous fall he had appeared on campus seemingly out of thin air. We learned he was from Indianapolis, but none of us knew him. He had done a stint in the US Air Force right out of high school, so he was older than most of us. Willie was tall, slender but trim, good looking, and a smooth talker. A prominent feature of his personality led him to often seek an edge over individuals and situations, even if it meant cutting a few corners. He was also chronically short on funds—that is, he was usually broke.

Willie drove a 1959 Chevrolet convertible that had seen its best days some time ago. After getting to know him, it became apparent that great academic achievement often eluded him. But he loved the fraternity. I suppose, despite his character flaws, that's why we kept him. However, he cut one too many corners.

Willie managed to achieve a passing GPA at the end of the fall semester. Assuming he continued to make his grades, he wanted be in the group of Scrollers to be initiated during the spring semester. We routinely checked all the Scrollers' official grade slips before the start of probation. At the time, grade reports were handwritten by the instructors. When I asked to see Willie's fall semester grade report, something looked amiss with his zoology grade, raising my suspicion that it might have been altered. I knew he was struggling in the course, so I questioned him about it. He told me he had not tampered with the grade slip and he had indeed achieved a C, which would give him a 2.0 GPA and allow him to be proceed with initiation. Still skeptical, I made an appointment with his instructor to determine the veracity of his claim. We met in his office the next day. When I presented Willie's grade report, the instructor had to review his grade book to confirm. Sitting beside him, I watched as he scanned the book until he came to Willie's name. It was a D. Willie had forged his grade slip.

Returning to the house, I confronted him with the information. "Willie, I paid a visit to Dr. Brenneman to confirm you passed zoology. You earned only a D, so this grade slip is wrong." He protested he had not tampered with the grade report, but I continued, "Well, someone did. Anyway, you didn't achieve a passing GPA, and the grade slip has been changed. Because of this you can't go over with your Scroller class."

He did not take it well, but he didn't protest further. By the end of the semester, his grades did not improve. He did not return in the fall.

One evening in mid-October, one of the pledges called me to the phone. I had a long distance call from the polemarch of our chapter at UCLA. We had never met; I had no clue why he wanted to speak with me. After introductions, he asked, "Do you know Willie Turner?"

"Yes," I replied, "why do you ask?"

It seemed during the summer Willie had made his way to Los Angeles, claimed he was a brother, and inserted himself into the Kappa chapter at UCLA. He told them that he had been initiated at Alpha chapter. Probably because he had no documentation and no one knew him, the chapter decided to check his credentials and found the Grand Chapter had no record of him. The polemarch wanted to know if Willie was telling the truth.

I explained that Willie had failed to achieve a passing GPA, so he was never initiated. The answer was no, he was not being honest. Next, Willie came to the phone and asserted he had indeed been initiated. I said it was simply not true. He related that Kenny Ellis, one of the older actives, had performed private initiation ceremony. I reiterated that whatever Kenny did or didn't do, none of it was official, so the bottom line was "Willie, you are not a Kappa."

I recounted what I had told Willie to the chapter polemarch. He thanked me, and that was it. I never learned what happened to Willie after our conversation.

There was another unanticipated and unwelcome outcome of the spring semester my sophomore year: my 2.6 GPA. Acutely aware of the tough subjects in the upcoming semester, coupled with my shaky GPA, I knew getting into medical school might be in jeopardy. After consulting with my counselor and my parents, and with Mr. Goodman's okay, I enrolled in two evening courses at the IU extension in Indianapolis for the summer session, finishing with an A and a B.

THIRTY-EIGHT

THE CHALLENGE OF THE DREAM

I WAS FORTUNATE TO return to the same job at Eli Lilly that summer. The racial dynamics were the same. The men in the crew had not changed either. A few days before I left to return to school, the Chief retired. The department supervisor hosted a retirement party in our lounge during lunch. At the end of the little ceremony, Chief was presented with a gold watch for his years of service. As the rest of us prepared to return to work, the White supervisor walked over to me, smiled patronizingly, and said, "You can come back here, and if you work hard you can receive the same thing, too!" I smiled without responding, but in my mind I said, "No fucking way!"

The high point of the summer of 1963 had nothing to do with my job, school, or my love life: it was the March on Washington on August 28, 1963. Publicity began weeks before its scheduled date. There was a great deal of apprehension about whether Dr. King and the other organizers could keep such a huge undertaking nonviolent. Those of us who remember the march also know that Dr. King was not the sainted figure he is today. That summer he was only thirty-four. Many young Black people loved him, but some, like those in the Student Nonviolent Coordinating Committee (SNCC), criticized him for not being aggressive enough. In contrast, many older African Americans, like my father, feared he was pushing too fast and too hard.

Malcolm X was at odds with Dr. King and his nonviolent tactics and condemned the march. My friends and I admired Dr. King, but we remained fearful the march might turn violent and of what the consequences might be if it did. Years later I learned that at the outset, the Kennedy administration, for some of the same reasons, was not in favor of the march, but after the president and his staff met with march leaders, and it was agreed there would be no civil disobedience, President Kennedy voiced his support. Though on the day of the march the temperature in Washington was in the eighties, it was an unusually pleasant August day in Indianapolis. CBS live-streamed the entire event. I was at work and unable to watch any of the television coverage. The other major networks covered it on their evening newscasts and specials.

At home, my habit was to sit cross-legged on the floor in front of the TV set. That evening, I settled into my usual spot while my mother sat in one of the chairs, and we watched the special coverage of the march following the six o'clock news. There were excerpts from several of the speakers who preceded Dr. King. He spoke last. His entire speech was telecast. What I remember most about the coverage were Mahalia Jackson's renditions of two spirituals and her shout out to Dr. King as he reached what was to be the climax of his speech: "Tell them about the dream, Martin!" Later we learned the most celebrated portion of his speech was unscripted. The soaring oratory in his "I Have a Dream" speech at the Lincoln Memorial, culminating in the "free at last" concluding segment, left the 250,000 in the crowd and my mother and me spellbound. I don't recall what my mother and I discussed at its conclusion. My father did not arrive home until later. I don't remember if we had a conversation about the event.

The following day, when my friends and I compared our assessments, we wondered if the march would have a favorable effect on the quest for civil rights legislation. We knew we would be able to vote in the presidential election the following year and were determined to sort out whom we should support.

From the perspective of almost sixty years later, I believe the success of the march and Dr. King's speech propelled him into a preeminent role in the civil rights movement. It is also credited with helping President Johnson get Congress to pass the Civil Rights Act the following year.

Year Three

1963–1964

THIRTY-NINE

"THOUGH WE CANNOT MAKE OUR SUN STAND STILL, YET WE WILL MAKE HIM RUN"

THE REMAINDER OF THE summer was uneventful. Soon it was time to return to school. Despite the turmoil of the previous year, I never lost sight of my goal of being accepted into medical school. Disappointing Mr. Goodman, my parents, and myself was not in the cards. I did not lose sight of my good fortune in not needing to worry about financing my education, although the cost of a college education had not escalated to its current level. In 1961, tuition was $7 per credit hour, which equates to $60.34 per hour today. A full load of fifteen credit hours for a semester would cost just over $900 in 2020. On the rare occasion someone asked how I was paying for college, I would respond, "I have a scholarship." If asked what kind of scholarship, I would only say, "It's a private scholarship." My discomfort was not in admitting my parents couldn't afford to send me to college, nor was it because Mr. Goodman was providing the funding. It was simply because I felt like I had not earned it.

My plan was to enter medical school after my junior year; the 1963–64 academic year would be my last in Bloomington. Having submitted all the application paperwork as well as scoring well on the Medical College Admission Test (MCAT) the previous spring, the in-person interview was the final step in the admission process. The first round of interviews usually took place in October. I wondered where I would fall in the queue.

To this point, I was assiduously following the path prescribed by my father. I was so immersed in the process of making his dream a reality I hadn't stopped to ask myself, "Why are you doing this? Is it just to please your father, or is it for yourself?" Answering this obvious question had eluded me until then. I searched for a synergy between the mantle placed on me by my father's expectations and Mr. Goodman's gift and my own desires. I realized the answer was medical school. It would fulfill everyone's goals.

Those with the greatest likelihood of being admitted—those with the highest MCAT scores and GPAs—were granted a first-round slot. Essentially all but one of my friends who were premed students had GPAs above 3.0. I didn't. Yet, like them, I was granted a first-round interview. You may ask how I managed to gain that slot with less than a 3.0 GPA. My score on the MCAT helped, but suffice it to say, I'm sure the fact that the chairman and several of the members of the IU Medical School Admissions Committee were my father's customers didn't hurt. His outsize personality, coupled with his shop's location in a downtown office building filled with physicians and attorneys, provided my dad with an extensive network of regular customers who were important and influential figures in the community. He was on a first-name basis with the mayor as well as the congressional delegation, but he was just as comfortable with the winos on the corner and the guys running numbers in the old neighborhood. So it wasn't surprising he would play a role in facilitating my path into medical school.

My most difficult course in the premed curriculum was physics in my junior year. It had not been a required subject in high school, so I hadn't taken it. The professor, Dr. Wilkinson, taught Physics 301 in the fall semester as well as Physics 302 the spring semester. I remember him for several reasons. First was his appearance. He was a diminutive man, short and skinny, who resembled a malnourished version of the actor Mickey Rooney. Reportedly, Dr. Wilkinson was a member of the Manhattan Project, which developed the first atomic bomb. His strangest quality really stood out. When he arrived in the lecture hall, it generated hissing, which he encouraged. He loved to be hated, and he was because the course was so difficult. One of the reasons became evident when he informed us at the first lecture that there would be only a single section of physics for the spring semester despite two sections of Physics 301. He actually said, "Look to your left and look to your right. One of you won't be here next semester." He wasn't kidding.

Just as he predicted, for the spring semester there was only one section of Physics 302. The exams were awful. Each consisted of two parts: first, a series of problems to solve with multiple choice answers. However, there were as many as twelve possible answers for each problem. To further complicate matters, he would work each problem, making all the common mistakes, and list those answers as well. You couldn't guess; you had to know how to correctly solve each one. The second portion consisted of a set of phrases linked by one of three words: *sometimes, always,* or *never.* He gleefully quipped, "Sometimes the answer is sometimes!"

Luckily, the exams were so difficult they were graded on a curve, but at the start of the semester even that wasn't enough to rescue me. Though I was able to achieve a C on the first quiz, for the first month the course completely baffled me. I did not understand the subject. On the day of the midterm exam, a month or so into the semester, I was already nervous, but once I looked at the test questions, I froze. Until that day I had never choked when taking an exam. Now, I simply stared at the questions for the first ten minutes, having no idea how to answer them. I left the exam room seriously unnerved. Two days later, when the graded tests were returned, I found I had messed up royally. I scored twenty out of one hundred. Even with the class average in the forties, twenty out of one hundred was still an F. All my Jewish buddies passed the exam. Fortunately, several of them had graduated from Shortridge with me and understood physics. I often studied with them at the ZBT or the SAM house. After the results of the midterm were returned, I spent a great deal more time with them.

How to get a passing grade in physics remained a monumental problem. Even as I began to understand the subject, my grade was not yet high enough to pass. The next exam was rumored to be the roughest of the semester, and I had to get at least a C. Though I had been a churchgoer for most of my life, at that point I did not consider myself deeply religious. But as the cliche "there are no atheists in foxholes" would predict, my prayers became a lot more fervent.

FORTY

WTF?

DISTRESS OVER PHYSICS CAUSED me to lose track of the date of my in-person medical school interview. Once the realization hit that this was the day, I had to rush from the main campus to the fraternity house, change clothes, then hurry back to the IMU to arrive on time. I didn't own a suit, so I wore dress slacks, a white shirt, and a tie, topped off with a rather loud blue madras blazer.

I arrived a few minutes before the appointment time. When I entered the waiting room, it seemed all the other interviewees were attired in conservative, dark-colored suits. The mood was somber. Apprehension, like the smoke from their cigarettes, lay heavy in the air. "Uh-oh!" I said quietly to myself. Self-conscious and feeling seriously out of place, I had no other option but to carry on.

When I was summoned, I discovered the two doctors who comprised my interview team were strange birds. Both were middle-aged White men who were professors in the Department of Microbiology. Dr. Edward Shrigley, who acted as the team's leader, was a stocky, round-faced, balding man with wire-rimmed glasses and an overbearing manner. The other, Dr. Sherman Minton, was quiet and bookish. He had a strong resemblance to Stan Laurel of the Laurel and Hardy comedy duo. I recall only the first set of questions. After introducing himself and his colleague and telling me to be seated, Dr. Shrigley, looking at me with a slightly patronizing smile, asked, "Do you know how to dance?"

I thought, "What?"

Haltingly I answered, "Yes, I do."

Next he mentioned a couple of the popular named dances—the Boogaloo was one of them—and asked, "Do you know how to do those dances?"

More than a little surprised he knew any of those dances existed, and chagrined at the question itself, again I answered, "Yes."

I had no clue where this line of questioning was headed, much less what any of it had to do with getting into medical school, but I was prepared to do a "Yessah, Boss" demonstration if it would get me admitted. Was this racial stereotyping because I was a Black man wearing a loud sport coat? Maybe. Was he a racist, since it was common knowledge IU's medical school had an unofficial quota system for African Americans? Possibly. I remember rising feelings of unease coupled with anger at what I thought were stupid questions. To this day, I have no explanation why he opened my interview that way, other than to believe it was an example of conscious or unconscious racial bias. Fortunately, he changed the line of questioning after that. Despite the rocky start, when I left the room at the conclusion of the interview, I felt I acquitted myself well.

FORTY-ONE

SEPTEMBER 19

AT THE BEGINNING OF each fall semester, one of the first priorities for us upperclassmen was surveying the female members of the incoming freshman class. During the first full week of the semester, a freshman girl from Florida, late of Kokomo, Indiana, named Gloria Francis entered my life. We met—where else?—in the Commons a few days after classes started. She was really cute, about five foot four, with a medium brown complexion and a great figure. But just as enticing as her appearance were her upbeat nature and zany personality. She was spontaneous, animated, and energetic, often speaking in a rapid-fire cadence punctuated with laughter that permeated throughout the room. She was typically at the center of any action, often singing a little off key to the tune being played on the jukebox. All these elements led me to want to know her better.

However, I cautioned myself against becoming involved in another romantic adventure, because I had entirely too many other things upon which I needed to concentrate. I really needed to focus on improving my grades to have a chance to be admitted into medical school. The fraternity was requiring a lot of my attention and time. As a consequence, I held back in pursuing her. But later, at her request, I called her, and we talked for over an hour and made a date for the next night. Curiously, this conversation occurred on September 19, a date I had always deemed special. As far as I could remember, nothing important had occurred on that date. Still, since childhood, for some unknown reason, I anticipated in the future something important would happen. This seemingly insignificant coincidence would prove prophetic. I had no notion this rather casual encounter would be the beginning of a relationship that would almost totally consume me for the next seven months.

The upcoming weekend featured two dances; Gloria and I went to both. I kissed her when we returned to her dorm at the end of our first date. The way she returned my kiss led me to think I aroused the same ardor in her as she generated in me. That weekend, her zany personality was in full bloom; I quickly became enamored with her, to the point of abandoning my pledge not to become involved with anyone.

As I was the president of Alpha chapter, the university considered me to be the face of the fraternity. In fact, I was also the leader of and responsible for a group of often unruly guys. At the outset, I felt I had to find a way to get the chapter back on the right track. It would begin with recruiting a new pledge class. We had a successful smoker and secured what appeared to be a good group that I hoped would result in raising the chapter's sagging grade point average.

Over the ensuing ten days, if Gloria and I didn't see one another we had daily phone conversations. I began to fall behind in my studies, but that didn't restrain me. Each time we got together, her actions and responses confirmed she really liked me. At the end of each evening, we joined the couples outside her dorm "ending the world." Clearly, she knew what she was doing. No one I dated had been so passionate in such a short time as Gloria! I loved it and was beginning to wonder if it was possible to fall in love in less than two weeks. However, I soon learned that my sense of finally being lucky in love was premature. It happened during a phone call.

"I need to tell you something," Gloria told me.

"Go ahead," I replied.

"I have a boyfriend in Kokomo, Mike Jessup."

"You do?"

"I thought I should tell you about him since he is planning to come down for homecoming weekend. We have been together for two years."

I wasn't prepared for this. After a taking a moment to let it sink in, I asked, "Do you love him?"

"Yes."

Totally confused, I couldn't fathom how Gloria could be so loving with me, then tell me she was in love with another guy. I didn't have a clue what I should do. While still on the call, I thought about it and saw two alternatives: stop seeing her now, or try to move ahead of Mike Jessup in her heart before homecoming weekend, a month away. My rational self told me to abandon the effort. I did not want to fall victim to loving and losing again. But the emotional part of me countered the rational self by encouraging me, despite great odds of failure, to stay in the game. I could tell Gloria cared for me, but what I thought was straightforward was now confusing and complicated. After all, we had dated for less than one month. Gloria waited patiently for my response.

"What do you think I should do?" I asked her.

"I don't know." After a pause, she added this caveat: "No matter what you decide to do, I want us to still be friends."

How she defined "friend" was a mystery, but asking me to transition from lover to friend sounded like taking a page from a paperback romance novel. Given the extent of my emotional involvement at the time, I felt it would be an impossible task.

"I will have to think about whether I can do that," I said.

The impact she made in my life in such a short time, notwithstanding the vow I made to myself, made me want more. The remainder of that day found me feeling seriously sorry for myself. By the next day, I decided I would try to do as she asked. I told her it was difficult for me to accept the change. It would be comparable to starting over with each of us hesitantly reaching out to the other, questioning how far to go. For the present, it was agreed we would continue to see each other. While I struggled to manage my emotional distress, Gloria seemed content and continued to act as if nothing had changed. She was just as affectionate as before. I didn't understand how she could carry on that way but decided to just go with it.

At the fraternity, there still were not enough of us to fill the house. Chapter finances had not improved. Each month began with the same ritual: our treasurer and I determined which creditors had to be paid first and which ones we could put off. Many times he or I would meet with a vendor to seek additional time to take care of our account. The chronic issue of some of the brothers and pledges failing to pay housing assessments on time had not been solved. Exasperated, though the house was filled to only one-half capacity, I announced to the delinquents: Pay up or move out! For a while, it helped.

Some of the brothers devised petty schemes that further contributed to the chapter's financial distress. In one of the more egregious examples, we had a pay phone installed on the main floor of the house. Having it cost the fraternity twenty-five cents a day. The price of a call was ten cents. It didn't take long before some of my more enterprising brothers developed a strategy to make a call and avoid paying the dime. A guy would call his girlfriend, let the phone ring twice, then hang up. His dime would be returned. That was code for her to call him right back. We lost money on the phone and eventually had it removed.

Over the next month the planned friendship between Gloria and me blossomed into a romance. She volunteered, "The process you're working on is happening, isn't it?" I don't remember telling her I would attempt to move past Mike in her heart, but by then it was obvious. Now certain I was falling in love, I believed she was falling for me too, which presented her with a dilemma. She wore a ring with the letter M on the fourth finger of her left hand. Once I learned its significance I told myself if she ever exchanged it for my class ring, I would be solidly in.

One evening, we stopped at the old Well House located in the middle of a lovely wooded grove in the heart of the central campus. I told her of the IU tradition called "making a coed" by kissing your girlfriend inside the Well House at midnight. She liked the idea, so at the stroke of midnight she officially became a coed. While she was still in my arms, I told her I was falling in love. I briefly considered offering my class ring to her then and there but decided it was too soon. She responded by saying the same was true for her, but neither of us had yet to say the words "I love you."

A week later, while out walking on a cool night in late October, we stopped at the Well House again, on Gloria's suggestion. Staring up at me, she said softly, "I love you, Lester." I was in heaven! I decided this was the time to offer her my class ring. At first she hesitated in accepting it, stating, "I want to, but it wouldn't be fair."

A bit confused over what she meant, but not wanting to force the issue, I responded, "That's okay."

There was a short silence, then she blurted out, "I want your ring, Lester!"

"Huh?"

"I want your ring. I want it!"

"Are you sure?"

"I love you, Lester!" She paused. "I know I love you, Lester. I know I do!"

Each time we saw each other after that evening, we always found places to do some serious making out. I knew Gloria was no longer a virgin, but I was too embarrassed to admit to her I still was. She quickly made it clear she was ready to take our relationship to a sexual level. I tried to conceal my nervousness when we agreed to stay out after hours and find a motel. My nervousness caused me forget to make a reservation earlier in the week. As luck would have it, that Friday night every motel was full. I couldn't take her back to the dorm. The only other alternative I could envision was to spend the night parked somewhere.

We ended up at Griffy Lake. It was a popular location for couples to indulge their passion. One notable item underscored why couples went there. On a low-hanging tree limb adjacent to a secluded spot along the shoreline where I chose to stop. a string of used condoms was displayed. Once there, my apprehension trumped my passion. I felt we couldn't have sex because of fear we would be discovered. This did not sit well with Gloria, but she grudgingly agreed. We spent the night there anyway.

The following weekend was homecoming. Despite having professed our love for one another, when I learned it was certain Mike was coming and Gloria was planning to meet him in Indianapolis on Thursday of the next week, it was comparable to throwing cold water onto our whole affair.

FORTY-TWO

THE BIG HURT

MY FRATERNITY WAS ONE of the many having a homecoming dance. Ours was on a Saturday night. By this time it was common knowledge Gloria and I were a couple. Things would become very awkward if she came to our dance with Mike. Her expression of "I love you, Lester" juxtaposed with attending our dance with my rival was going be hard to accept emotionally. I also worried the impact would make me appear to be a sucker. Despite the terrible outcome I anticipated, I had to concede this weekend to Mike. She may not have loved him more than me, but she had loved him longer.

Friday night came and went with no sign of Gloria and Mike, but on Saturday night they walked into the Kappa house. Mike and I had never met. Despite being warned, I had no strategy planned to deal with this incursion. As I struggled with my emotions, I must have looked lost. Early in the evening, separately, two of Gloria's friends, one of whom was a longtime friend of mine, approached me and said basically, "Stop lying back. If you want this girl, get in there and go after her with the best you have." Their words were a wake-up call. Realizing if I was to woo Gloria away from Mike, it would require more than simply saying "I love you." I told myself, "To hell with Mike" and for the latter half of the dance spent as much time with Gloria as I could. Taking her friends' advice, I took Gloria aside and told her I trusted the time we spent together demonstrated my devotion, but if she felt pride and ego made me complacent, she needed to know how deeply I cared for her and how much she meant to me. She was visibly moved as she said softly, "I love you, Lester." We held each other's gaze for a few seconds, then she had to go.

Until this weekend, I had believed my words and actions placed me in the lead in the battle for her heart. Considering what was transpiring in front of me, I had to wonder, did she simply not know which of us she wanted, or did she love me only when Mike was not there? I chose to believe the former possibility and was determined to make the choice obvious to her. Surprisingly, though Mike must have noticed, he didn't appear upset but seemed to be enjoying the company of several other girls. This left me to conclude this dude was really a player, or he thought my efforts wouldn't alter the equation.

This weekend signaled the end of our beginning. Thereafter, I attempted to make a greater effort, not only tell Gloria but also to show her how much I loved her. To emphasize the point, I wrote this poem dedicated to her.

She Comes before Me

When I think of her, I see
Waves surging toward sunlit shores.
Within my heart I do adore her
And I will love her more.

When I think of her, I get a feeling,
A new sensation, so warm, yet strange
It whispers soft in its revealing
That I love her.

When I think of her, I can't help smiling
Into her eyes, so large and full.
Her lovely eyes, so beguiling,
So I must love her.

When I think of her, my heart shines through me.
Spreading its rays much like the sun,
So that whate'r the world does to me
She knows I love her.

When I think of her, thoughts beyond telling
Of how I long to have her near.
From deep within me thoughts come welling
Of how I love her. She is the one.

When I think of her there is no sadness,
No evil thoughts within me lie.
Just the glow of eternal gladness
Of how I love her.

The first time we saw each other at the beginning of the following week, I recited it for her. After hearing me read it, she gushed out, "It's beautiful!" Then she asked how I happened to pick that one. She was amazed when I told her I wrote it. Today, I see my passion outstripped my talent. It is not great verse, but it did reflect how I felt at the time.

We planned to stay out the upcoming weekend to finish what we had begun that night at Griffy Lake. Finally, the night I anticipated arrived. About to lose my virginity, I was wildly excited and nervous, but without any prior sexual experience I did not know exactly what to expect or, except for the obvious, exactly what to do. It was a serious disappointment my first experience wasn't what I'd thought it would be. I put on the condom and proceeded to undress and kiss and fondle her, which quickly triggered mutual arousal. After embracing her for a few minutes, I eased in with a couple of jerks. All of a sudden, whoosh! I felt a rush of heat as we started undulating. The orgasm came before I knew it. Its onset was so rapid, I couldn't restrain myself; I didn't know how. The rest of the act was me working hard (no pun intended) trying to maintain my erection. Yet with all my effort, I couldn't satisfy her. I was disgusted and embarrassed. Gloria still perceived me as an accomplished lover. I confessed I lacked experience, but she wouldn't buy it. She said, "You do the before too well not to know what to do after that." I still couldn't admit to her this was my first time. I just couldn't.

But what hurt us both was that once again I had failed to plan ahead and brought only one condom. There were no twenty-four-hour drugstores in Bloomington. I wouldn't have sex again without one. Gloria begged me, "Oh, come on, please. It's okay." It required all my strength not to give in, but I didn't dare take the chance. I was determined to be better next time.

FORTY-THREE

THE END OF CAMELOT

GLORIA AND I AGREED we would stay out again the next weekend, but that Friday was November 22, 1963, the day President Kennedy was assassinated. For all of us who are old enough to remember it, the date and its events are seared into our memories. America came to a standstill; our country's innocence died with him. The news came to me when a voice over the intercom speaker during my German class delivered this message: "The president has been shot!" Soon the news of his death flooded the airwaves. I retreated to the Commons, where I discovered many of my friends had already gathered. We were distraught; many were crying, not only because of the assassination but over the fact that Lyndon Johnson, a Southern Democrat, was now the president. He was not known to be a friend to Black folks. All over the Commons there was a great deal of woe is me-ing, angst, and tears. What follows are excerpts from my journal over the ensuing three days based on what we knew at the time.

It's nearly impossible for me to express just what I feel. A deep-seated pain, it is the hurt of hopelessness and uncertainty, the anguish of disbelief and bewilderment, the helpless feeling of knowing yet not knowing. Phrases like "I don't believe it" or "It couldn't happen" are heard everywhere. I can't believe that John Kennedy, the president of the United States, is dead! He was shot in the early afternoon while riding in an open car with Mrs. Kennedy, the governor of Texas, and his wife in a motorcade driving through the streets of Dallas on a campaign tour. He was hit in the head. Immediately, he slumped into the arms of his wife, who cried, "Oh God, he's been shot!" There may have been a second shot. The governor of Texas was also critically wounded. Vice President, now President Johnson was, I think, in a separate car and was not hurt. Kennedy was rushed to the nearest hospital, his head in his wife's lap. He died there about one-half hour later. His wound was described by doctors as "massive." He could not have been saved. The rifle was found on the fifth floor of a book depository building along the route. Three shells had been fired; one was still in the chamber. Acting on a tip, the Dallas police nabbed a suspect who killed a policeman during his arrest in a movie theater. He is Lee Harvey Oswald, twenty-four years old. He was quoted as saying, "It's all over now." It's not clear if he was the only assassin. I'm forced to believe this whole thing was carefully planned. Though I didn't know or especially like the president, I admired and respected him. Mrs. Kennedy is the one I really feel sorry for. She's a strong woman to maintain her composure. She comes to Dallas sitting next to her husband. About four hours later, she is on her way back to Washington on the same plane with her husband in a casket. That is a bitch!

The following day: "Somebody shot Oswald!" I hurried downstairs to the TV room where the news flash was being telecast. The incident was captured live. As Oswald was being led out of the police station to be put into a van, a man named Jack Ruby approached, drew a pistol, and fired. He was immediately disarmed and arrested. An hour later, Oswald died in the same hospital as President Kennedy, only two doors down the hall from the room where Kennedy had expired. To this day, many questions about those events remain unanswered. Was there a conspiracy behind the president's assassination? If so, who was behind it? Was Oswald killed to keep him from talking? Or was it just as coincidental as it seemed? As my fraternity brothers and I watched this scenario unfold, Freddie Stewart told us a Bahai prophesy indicated the year 1963 would bring about great changes. At that moment, it seemed the prophecy had been fulfilled.

We were once again glued to our TV as Kennedy's casket was moved to the Rotunda of the Capitol Building, where the public could view it. We watched as Mrs. Kennedy and her daughter, Caroline, walked slowly up to the casket and knelt. Jackie tenderly kissed the flag draped over it. Caroline also kissed it. Then they rose and walked away.

FORTY-FOUR

HOORAY! I'M IN!

BEFORE THE AFOREMENTIONED PHYSICS exam was scheduled, the medical school acceptance letters for the first-round interviewees arrived by mail. Several times on the day they were delivered, I crossed paths with my fellow first-round interviewees who had already received their acceptance letters. Each one asked if I had received one. Although I regarded almost all of my Jewish premed brethren to be smarter than me, they treated me as an equal. I appreciated their vote of confidence, but at times I felt like an imposter. I responded that I had not returned to the house since I'd left in the morning, so I didn't know.

We didn't have individual mailboxes in the Kappa house; the mail was usually dumped in a pile on a bench in the foyer. Upon arriving home, my anxious search of the remaining mail disclosed no letter. Suddenly, I flashed back to the day when the cut list for the freshman high school basketball tryouts was posted. Fighting back tears, I was crushed!

Almost immediately, I began to rationalize my situation. Since the letter *T* was toward end of the alphabet, perhaps the letter wouldn't come until the following day. That theory didn't fly because I had friends whose last names began with letters further down the alphabet who had received them. Next, I began to wonder what happened. Was I wait-listed or simply not accepted?

For the remainder of the evening, I was adrift with no plan for what to do if I hadn't been accepted. About ten o'clock, there was a knock at my door. It was Howard Carson, one of the pledges. In his hand was a registered letter addressed to me that had arrived earlier in the day. I wasn't there, so he signed for it but forgot to give it to me. I almost ripped the letter from his hand and opened it. Yep, it was the acceptance letter from IU's med school. Hallelujah! I was in! Surprisingly, I don't remember any details of my parents' or Mr. Goodman's reaction when I shared the news with them. I can guess all three were supremely proud. But I still had to pass physics.

Despite my struggles with physics, as the semester progressed, something within me kept saying not to worry. This "something" was not a vision nor a voice from on high but merely an awareness, a feeling. Though totally irrational, it was so prominent I began to capitalize the *F* in the word *feeling* in my journal entries when I referred to it. Was it God? I never received an answer to the question. If it was a message from God, divine intervention did not come right away.

Two weeks before the big test, becoming increasingly desperate, I scheduled an appointment to see Dr. Wilkinson to seek his help in improving my understanding of the course and thereby my grade. We met in his office. To my surprise, one on one, in contrast to his lecture persona, he was not at all intimidating but very empathetic and willing to offer help. He pointed out where I was falling short in my studying routine and provided me with helpful tips to improve my understanding and my grade. I was immensely grateful. With his advice, finally understanding what I was doing, a lot of intense studying coupled with good luck, and possibly a little divine intervention, I managed to pass the exam with a B and the course with a C. The Feeling was right! At the start of Physics 302, I figured out how to successfully navigate my way and finished the semester with another C. It was enough to keep my admission into medical school intact.

FORTY-FIVE

THE 24 HOUR GRILL

THE KAPPA HOUSE WAS, in a way, like a watering hole in the savanna because it attracted all sorts of active and inactive brothers. Chapter leaders let the inactive members continue to participate in fraternity activities under the guise of brotherhood and all that. It made no sense. I said to myself, "If we continue to allow them to stay involved, what is the incentive for them to become active again?" None, so far as I could see. I was determined this had to stop.

In late October, we had a Friday night beer blast. Three inactive brothers wanted to take part, and I told them they could not. There was resistance, but I prevailed, and grudgingly they left. Some of the other actives were not happy, but I didn't care. This conflict escalated as we geared up for the next probation week.

By this time I had become convinced that the intensity and amount of physical hazing was wrong and had to be stopped or, at the very least, reduced. I couldn't garner enough support to end it altogether. When I unveiled my idea for modifications at a chapter meeting, it was not enthusiastically received. I found the wall surrounding the chapter's customs was too high for me to surmount. For three hours we debated what we should do. In the end, not everyone agreed with my plan to decrease the amount of physical punishment, but a sufficient number did to make it happen.

It was a chilly evening in late November. I had returned to the house from the Hole and was already in bed when Steve Talley rushed into the dorm shouting, "Get up! Do you want to help Mike and OB?" OB was the nickname of Charles O'Bannion "They're in trouble at the 24 Hour Grill!"

"What? What happened?" I questioned.

"They've been jumped by some stone cutters." Limestone is abundant in southern Indiana. At the time, there were several active quarries near Bloomington. Those who worked the quarries were typically working-class White men. They were called stone cutters by the locals. Southern Indiana was a region of entrenched racism dating back to the date of the state's first constitution in 1816. Most often these men fit that mold, so to us the terms *stone cutter* and *redneck* were synonymous. After a few seconds of indecision, I leaped out of bed and shouted, "Let's go!"

By the time I had gotten into my pants, the entire house was rallying. The awareness that we might have to do some fighting was apparent. There were eight to ten of us between Steve's and Reuben's cars. Wayne McCoy was loading a third car. On the way, I wanted to know what had happened. Someone said OB and Mike had called for help. There had been a fight. No longer did I have any doubt we would have to go to war!

When we pulled up across the street from the grill, there were several White boys standing in an adjacent parking lot. A few feet away were our guys. Insults flew back and forth—we called it "woofing." Shouts of "motherfuckers" and "niggers" filled the air. As we walked across the street to rescue our friends, I was shaking like a leaf, partially because it was a cold night, but mostly from being scared. When we reached the other side, several more White guys arrived in the parking lot. The first group had called in reinforcements. I thought, "These are some hard-looking peckerwoods"—another derogatory term for a redneck. I glanced back to the opposite side of the street just as Reuben's and Wayne McCoy's cars were unloading.

For the first few minutes, as the two reinforced groups confronted each other, there was only verbal taunting with both groups selling lots of "wolf tickets." I hoped someone had called the cops and they would show up before any real violence started. They did, but it had no effect. Two White policemen exited the squad car. One cop directed us to leave. Everyone in our group protested, demanding everyone should leave the scene; we stood our ground. Then the cop threatened just us with arrest. Before he could act, two more policemen arrived: a uniformed officer and a short, squatty detective. During this brief pause, one of the White guys challenged "the toughest guy in the group" to fight him. Pointing to Lobo, who had appeared since we arrived, the guy said, "Do you want to fight?"

The cops just stood there. Then one said, "Don't fight here. Go back into the alley." A great move from the local gendarmes!

Lobo replied, "Yeah, I'll fight you, you motherfucker!"

"You've got big lips," the stone cutter sneered.

As people started crowding around those two, the cops stood silent.

"Your mama's got big lips," Lobo retorted.

With that, the White guy threw a punch and missed. Lobo downed him with four or five punches then dropped on top of him, and the pummeling continued. We tried to hold the others back. The officers still took no action. Suddenly, another White guy charged in from the crowd and leaped onto Lobo's back, sucker punching him. Immediately, I saw Cameron Lee's (one of our guys) red shirt flash by and land on top of the second assailant, soon followed by someone jumping on top of him. The first guy was trying to escape, but O'Bannion, Talley, Harold, and Reuben were on him, kicking the shit out of him. Several more fights broke out. I figured this was it, so I removed my glasses and prepared to defend myself if attacked. The next thing I knew, Lobo was lying on the ground in front of me, with one of the White guys saying, "Leave him alone! Don't touch him! He's out cold."

At that, the fighting stopped. A couple of minutes later, Lobo woke up and managed to get to his feet. Finally the cops acted. A thought flashed into my head: "What if I get arrested?" The second policeman who arrived with the detective told us, "You boys leave now. Come down to the station later and press charges. I'll be on the desk."

He smiled and shook my hand. His reaction seemed strange given the scenario we had just witnessed, but we agreed. I began rounding up our guys, which wasn't easy. The cops also told the group of White guys to leave the area. Fighting almost broke out again before we left. It took four of us to put one of our brothers, Mike Johnston, into McCoy's car. On the way back to the house, I found out how it all had begun.

After leaving the Hole and finding no other place open, Rosie, Cameron Lee, Mike, and OB went to the 24 Hour Grill to get something to eat. They ordered burgers and planned to eat outside since it was a notorious stone-cutter place, and they knew they would not be welcome inside. In retrospect, going there at all was a foolish decision. Back in the parking lot, after they received their food, a '51 Chevy containing several White guys roared into the lot, almost striking Cameron. He shouted at them, "What's the matter with you!?"

Three guys jumped out of the car. Another one came out of the grill. By happenstance, Lobo had just arrived from across the street. Heated words were passed between both groups, and then a fight broke out. A few moments later, the cops arrived and stopped the fighting, but tensions continued to build. No arrests were made, and the police left after making a threat about what they would do if they had to return. Fighting broke out again, this time between Lobo and one of the White guys. During the scuffle, the same cop returned, and once again the fighting stopped. Still, he took no action and departed a second time. Meanwhile, the White guys had sent for reinforcements. That was when OB called us.

Back at the house, we patched up Lobo, and then Rosie, McCoy, Steve, and I drove to the Bloomington police station. We described the events leading up to our arrival to the policemen. We were terribly frustrated by the lack of action at the scene by the Bloomington police force. It left us with the opinion that the last two officers with whom we'd dealt were the only good cops on the force. The rest, from our experience, were useless.

I, along with Steve and Rosie, signed complaints against our assailants. The two most aggressive ones were well known to the department. They were the notorious Stagg brothers, who had just been released from jail. The one who sucker punched Lobo had killed a man in a fight, no less! Shot him. Captain Cox and Deputy Hernandez from IU security had been called to the station and were filled in on what had occurred. No one of our group was charged. Exhausted, we left the station about four o'clock in the morning.

I still wonder if the lack of action by the Bloomington policemen was a reflection of implicit racial bias. Given the time frame, the location, and the particulars of the incident, I believe it was. Today we would label the assault as a racially motivated hate crime. Whatever you want to call it, it was the first time I felt in physical danger in Bloomington. I never mentioned anything about this episode to my parents or to Mr. Goodman.

Nevertheless, despite the somber mood after the altercation, fraternity boys will still be silly. A few days later, some of the pledges tried to throw Steve into the showers. I jumped in to help him, and they grabbed me too. They managed to get my feet aimed toward the showers. OB and a second pledge made the mistake of standing with their backs to the open shower stalls with the water running, each holding one of my legs. With one sudden, strong kick from me, both went into a shower stall, but I didn't. In retaliation, we locked the pledges out of the house for the night.

FORTY-SIX

REALLY?

AS THE FALL SEMESTER continued to play out, trying to apportion the appropriate amount of time to schoolwork, social life, and the fraternity was becoming a serious problem. I was failing physics, jeopardizing the expectations of Mr. Goodman and my parents. Gloria and I were becoming serious. The fraternity seemed to be going to hell for a variety of reasons. We continued the "creative management plan" to deal with our debts. The struggle to pay the chapter's bills was all too familiar to me. It was the same method my father had employed with our family finances as I was growing up. The insecurity was unnerving. I vowed when I grew up I would never have to worry about paying my bills.

One fall weekend after the Thanksgiving break, during a particularly difficult period, my father drove to the campus to visit me. I can't remember exactly why. The two of us were in my study room when he asked, "How are you doing now that you are the chapter president?" I began to explain the fraternity's financial straits and my efforts to deal with them. Before I could go into specifics, he interrupted me, trivializing the problems: "Boy, you don't know anything about dealing with financial trouble." I reacted angrily to his dismissive attitude and proceeded to give him chapter and verse of the maneuvers I employed just to keep the house afloat. It must have hit home because he listened without further interruption. My dad loved to brag to his friends and customers about his son's accomplishments, but rarely did he compliment me directly. When I finished, all he said was, "I didn't know that." It was my validation.

It was close to Christmastime, and the holiday break was rapidly approaching. Before everyone left for home, I gave the Scrollers a task. My charge was to get a tree, place it in front of the picture window in the living room, and trim it. I didn't give them any instructions on where to find a tree or any funds to buy it. I told them to use their resourcefulness.

A day or two later, I returned to the house in the early evening. Entering the front door, I was confronted by a huge fir tree lying in the foyer. It had been snowing. The melting snow from the tree formed a large puddle on the slate floor. No pledges were in sight. After a short search, I located a Scroller and asked where the tree came from and why it was left lying in the foyer. Initially, he pleaded ignorance. Finally, another one of the Scrollers sheepishly came forward and described how the tree was obtained.

Rather than asking for the money or pooling theirs and purchasing a tree, the Scrollers decided to steal one. There were several huge fir trees growing just a few feet from the rear of the Phi Delta Theta fraternity house. Their house was only a few hundred yards away from the south side of Seventeenth Street, directly visible through the picture window of our living room. Once it was dark, they cut one down. To make matters worse, not only did they steal the tree, but they then dragged it through the snow across Seventeenth Street, up our driveway, and into the house. Once they brought it inside, someone must have realized what they had done as well as the possible consequences of a trail in the snow leading up to our house and a large tree suddenly appearing in our living room. It didn't require a great intellect to figure out what might happen if the Phi Delts followed the trail. So they just left it lying in the foyer.

There was no specific bad blood between us and the Phi Delts; we were not, however, friends. Their members were all White and mostly jocks. The frat had a national reputation of repeated episodes of destructive hell-raising. After hearing this, I couldn't believe the Scrollers had not been caught and that they could be that stupid! We never put the tree up.

FORTY-SEVEN

THE STORM BECOMES A HURRICANE

THE RIFT BETWEEN THE old-school brothers, primarily Rosie and Kenny, and me regarding how I was running the fraternity and the approaching probation never disappeared and grew wider. A feeling of disillusionment enveloped me as we were once again conducting another probation. As I noted, my goal was to reduce the physical hazing. Other than that, I didn't care.

The old-school Kappas, led by Rosie, continued sniping at the process and at me. None of them liked the way pro was being conducted. They believed the institutionalized brutality was close to sacred. My desire was simply to get through the week. All but Rosie were inactive; their opinions didn't matter. Why I allowed them to participate at all is still a mystery. The climax came on turn-back night. I understood the way we conducted it had become a tradition, but this "tradition" was nothing more than tribal law. The powerful pull of tradition prevented me from eliminating the segment altogether, but I stopped it at what would have normally been the halfway point.

Rosie entered the room when I announced my decision and erupted, shouting it was a sacrilege to discontinue crossing the sands early! Not anticipating his broadsided attack, I was blindsided by it. When Rosie turned against me, it was terribly disappointing because he had been my friend and mentor. Disregarding his objections, I stood firm and ended it. After the confrontation, the rift, now a chasm, destroyed what remained of our friendship. When it was over, distressed and not knowing what would happen next, I sought counsel with Freddie. He agreed I was right in shutting things down, adding he thought the primary cause of my disillusionment stemmed from trying too hard to right every wrong. I was jousting with too many windmills. The following night, the going-over dance went on without a hitch. Rosie and I left IU at the end of the school year. Though we never saw one another again, it took twenty years for me to forgive him.

As luck would have it, the start of the Stagg brothers' assault trial coincided with our final exam week. Along with several others, I was subpoenaed by Mr. Hornaday, the prosecutor, to provide witness testimony. He summoned us to his office the evening before the trial was to begin to go over our testimony and the trial procedures. Just being there made me nervous.

Our first day in court was a Friday. We—Steve, Mike J., Rosie, OB, McCoy, Lobo, C. Lee, and I—spent the entire day in court. One of the first defense motions was to sequester the witnesses. The judge granted the motion, so we were sent to a side room to wait to be called. I noted in my journal the courthouse building was old and drab; the witness room was sparsely furnished with old tables and several uncomfortable wooden chairs. At least it was sufficiently quiet, so we were able to study for our upcoming exams.

I was not called to testify until day two. The prosecutor called me as his first witness and had me describe what occurred. During cross-examination, the defense counsel attempted to get me to acknowledge that our arrival had initiated the fight. I was adamant that we'd come only to retrieve our friends. The trial lasted for four or five days, but we were allowed to leave the witness room to take our exams and then return. Both Stagg brothers were convicted.

FORTY-EIGHT

THE LAST DANCE

IN 1960, NANCY WILSON erupted onto the jazz scene. By 1962, she had become a star. All of us loved her music. Typically, we partied to rock and roll and rhythm and blues. But after hours, the music switched to jazz. Nancy was our favorite female jazz singer, plus she was only four or five years older than us.

On tour with another of our favorite musicians, Cannonball Adderley and his band, Nancy was appearing in Indianapolis for two nights. I was able to secure two tickets to the first of the two shows on Sunday night. Gloria didn't know the members of Cannonball Adderley's band, but when I gave her their names she told me her aunt was once engaged to his bass player, Sam Jones. Hearing that, I had an idea! I suggested we make an attempt to meet him backstage; perhaps we could also meet Cannonball and maybe Nancy as well.

We composed a letter of introduction. Once we arrived at the venue, I bribed an usher to take the letter backstage to Sam Jones. We asked if he would be willing to meet us after the performance. Our luck held when he came out after the first show and invited us backstage. Then Gloria took the ball and ran with it! As he led us downstairs to the dressing room, he and Gloria talked about her aunt back in Florida, also Sam's home state, and their families. Once in the dressing room, we met Cannonball, and he introduced us to his bandmates as well as the performers who opened the show. Cannonball was gracious and impressed us as a genuine guy. We conversed for several minutes.

Then Gloria asked Sam if we could meet Nancy. He didn't think so, but he motioned for her to follow him to see if she was available. She disappeared

163

while I continued to talk with Cannonball and his keyboardist, Joe Zawinul. Joe was from Vienna. Though he spoke fine English, my German course allowed us to also converse a bit *auf Deutch*. He was quite surprised to hear this skinny Black kid speaking the language! A few minutes later, Gloria returned, led by Nat, Cannonball's younger brother and the trumpeter in the band. He was taking us to Nancy's dressing room to meet her!

"I'll tell her you're my cousin," he said to Gloria.

We reached the door as Nancy walked out.

"I'd like you to meet my cousin," Nat began.

"You have a cousin here?" Nancy asked.

"I've got relatives all over the world!"

There she stood, stunningly attractive in a red-orange dress and heels. Sweet Nancy! I anticipated she would be aloof, simply greeting us politely and that would be that. On the contrary, she was very open and greeted us warmly with graciousness. By her manner, she still seemed awed by her success. After introducing us to friends in her dressing room, all by first names, we talked for five to ten minutes more until it was almost time for the second show. As we were about to leave, she asked if we had to hurry back to school since it was Sunday. We said no, so she invited us to watch the second show from the wings. We did. Talk about wow! Afterward we thanked them all, said our goodbyes, and left, arriving back on campus about two o'clock in the morning. Gloria managed to sneak back into her dorm without being detected.

As special as it was, this night was the final act of our romance. The fact that Mike was not in Bloomington didn't matter; he didn't need to be. Soon afterward, it became clear that no matter how much Gloria cared for me, Mike was the one she really wanted. He won. I lost. As I sadly witnessed the demise of our love affair, it became clear whatever Gloria needed was something I could not provide. From that point, our encounters were mostly awkward and uncomfortable. My first passionate love affair had finally come to an end. As I left for home at the end of the semester, I thought it likely I would not hear from her again.

A year later, I was one of her old friends invited to her wedding when she married Mike. Another year passed. I was nearing the end my summer quarter externship at Methodist Hospital in Indianapolis. The third year of medical school was soon to begin. Each extern had a mailbox in the hospital's Medical

Education Office. When I checked mine at the end of the day, inside I found an official medical staff envelope addressed to me. As I opened the envelope, I thought, "I wonder what this is about."

Inside I found a typed note. Because it was in a hospital envelope, the note must have been hand delivered. The office staff had left, so there was no one to ask about who had brought it. It read, "Lester, I have something to talk to you about. Will call you Friday. Love, Gloria." After reading it, I said out loud to no one, "Hmm, today is Friday." I never received a call.

FORTY-NINE

BRANCHING OUT

DURING MY TIME IN Bloomington, I saw my fraternity's social relationship with the Jewish fraternity Sigma Alpha Mu (the Sammies) as a natural outcome of how many Jews allied with African Americans during the early days of the Civil Rights Movement. I wanted to broaden that relationship. So, despite all the difficulties Alpha chapter was experiencing, in the early fall of my year as polemarch we cosponsored a dance with the Sammies. It was the first time the two frats had joined in hosting an event of any sort. I was curious to see how it would turn out.

We agreed to split the cost of the live band, Arne Goldberg and the Soul Brothers. It was an interesting moniker for a group of Jewish musicians. Arne was a student; he and his band were often booked for campus dances. The group cut a record, "The Prune," which became a local hit and the band's signature tune. The dance was scheduled to start at 8:00 p.m. in our parking lot. At the risk of pushing another stereotype too far, most of us were not accustomed to showing up at social events at the opening bell. To our great surprise, this was not true for the Sammies, who arrived right at eight o'clock.

Despite the slow start, it quickly turned into serious party time! I was asked to sing "Zum Gali" a cappella. I had sung that tune so many times, it was easy. I should have stopped there, but ego and ambition took over and I decided to sing a tune accompanied by Arne's band. Mind you, I had never sung with a band. We had not rehearsed any numbers. I asked Arne if the band could play "Summer Time" from *Porgy and Bess*. He indicated they could. We picked the key, and I began to sing. I found it much harder than singing a cappella. My performance did not flow well, but I received some polite applause anyway. Score another one for ego over judgment.

That year we also broadened our involvement in the greater university community. One pathway for interfraternity cooperation was through athletics. Several of the Kappas were skilled basketball players. Our most dominant player was Earl Faison, a two-sport college athlete who was the reigning rookie of the year in the American Football League. Earl was a defensive lineman and one huge dude at six feet five and 270 pounds. He had left IU early to play in the AFL, then returned to complete his degree. In the final game of the fraternity championship, we played the Phi Delta Theta team, also primarily composed of jocks. Early in the game, Earl suffered a knee injury that put him out. We lost. Though it was a Black versus White team competition, things went along smoothly.

I'm also proud to note we added another campus event to our schedule. Each spring, the Tau Kappa Epsilon fraternity, known as the Tekes, sponsored a campuswide chariot race for charity. Many of the frats and some of the dorms entered teams consisting of four guys pulling a homemade chariot with a sweetheart (usually a very small girl) riding in it. It was a 100-yard dash. Team members wore costumes, usually with either Roman or Egyptian themes. The Kappas had never entered a team. I thought it was a pretty good idea and would be fun. We constructed a chariot, dressed four burly football players in Roman togas, and added a tiny AKA sister, who was a similarly attired, as our damsel. We acquitted ourselves pretty well by winning our heat and finishing fifth overall. We also secured a third-place award for our costumes.

Despite these forays into greater campus life, most of the members of our social group did not take part in campuswide activities. The anecdote below illustrates one of those situations and our thoughts about it.

I was our chapter's representative to the Interfraternity Council (IFC). The IFC joined the Intersorority Council to sponsor an all-Greek dinner for the representatives from each house. With only five Black Greek organizations on campus, our representatives were always greatly outnumbered by their White counterparts. As a group, these organizations were our only formal interaction with the White Greeks. As creatures of habit, we sat together at the table, three on one side facing two on the opposite side. To our surprise, the entrée was fried chicken. Self-consciously staring at our plates, we wondered if the food choice had anything to do with the fact that we were in attendance.

Once everyone was served, we noticed no one had begun to eat. Maybe this was paranoia, but when a couple of minutes had elapsed with no movement, we glanced at one another and we concluded the others were waiting to see whether we ate our chicken using a knife and fork or with our hands. I remember hearing one of the two girls in our group saying, "I know only one way to eat fried chicken" as she picked up a drumstick. With the ice broken, everyone else followed suit.

In similar situations, we always saw the eight-hundred-pound gorilla of race in the room, but I'm not at all sure our White counterparts did. Those situations often produced a subtle sense of discomfort, a feeling of being patronized rather than accepted. One might think the cumulative impact of small incidents such as this one might stimulate a dialogue with our White counterparts about the racial climate on campus. But to my knowledge, it didn't. I recall us laughing about what happened as we left the event.

Even when a White classmate came to the Kappa house for a study session, we never talked about race. One evening I was studying in my room with John Stewart, a fellow premed student and a guy from a small town in southern Indiana, when a loud cry came from the hallway: "Nigger!" I quickly looked over at John to gauge his reaction, prepared to start a conversation about what he had just heard. He didn't flinch; there was no conversation. I recall only a couple of late-night, in-depth discussion sessions with two of my close Jewish friends. Looking back, I wish we had them a lot more often. Outside of the classroom, we Black students functioned mostly within our own social network.

FIFTY

LITTLE GEORGE

NINETEEN SIXTY-FOUR WAS A presidential election year. The upstart seg-regationist governor of Alabama, George Wallace, announced his candidacy for President. He entered the Indiana primary as a Democrat and came to IU to deliver a campaign speech. This was the same George Wallace who, in June of 1963, stood in the doorway of the University of Alabama to block the admission of two Black students. A group of us decided to protest his visit by picketing outside the auditorium during the speech.

A couple of weeks before his April 24 visit, we agreed on our strategy and prepared protest signs. The only slogan I remember was our paraphrase of the Indianapolis Motor Speedway's slogan: "The Greatest Spectacle in Racing." We modified it to "The Greatest Spectacle in Racism." The morning of his speech, we joined the crowd assembled outside the auditorium and filed in. Once inside, we waited a few minutes after he had begun to speak, then silently stood up, turned toward the exit, walked out, picked up our signs, and began our protest. The age of disruptive, confrontational protest demonstra-tions had not yet arrived on the IU campus.

Both local and national news organizations covered the speech and the protest, but I didn't see any of us on the evening newscasts. I knew one of the students involved with bringing Wallace to the campus. Almost on a whim, a day or two before his arrival, I told this student we would like to invite Gov-ernor Wallace to dinner at the Kappa house so we could talk with him. He laughed, thinking I was joking, but was shocked when I told him I was serious.

He agreed to pass the invitation on to the governor. If he accepted, I figured we'd make the CBS six o'clock news with Walter Cronkite! When I told the brothers about my invitation, it created a huge stir. Mrs. Brooks, our cook, who was from Alabama, asked me, "You invited Little George to dinner? I'll poison him!"

I told her that would be bad form. Wallace declined the invitation, allegedly because he had to leave the campus right after the speech. I learned he was scheduled to speak in Indianapolis later the same day, but I doubt that was the only reason he declined.

FIFTY-ONE

THE MUSIC MAN FROM MEMPHIS

IN APRIL IT WAS time to initiate another group of pledges. It would be the last initiation in which I would participate. Since the conflict over the end of the previous fall's probation, the division between the old guard and the rest of us was kept mainly under wraps and didn't resurface as we approached this one. I was able to eliminate the physical hazing. On turn-back night I once again cut the burning sands segment in half; it was, at best, only an incremental improvement. I wished I had the ability to stop it entirely.

One of the new brothers was a young musician who would be destined for greatness. Booker T. Jones arrived on campus from Memphis in September of 1962 at age seventeen. We were familiar with his name because of the hit record "Green Onions," released earlier that year by his group, Booker T. and the MGs. A look at the album cover revealed something quite unusual—the band was integrated. Two of its four members were White. Given his name, we were certain that Booker was not one of the two White guys, but we didn't know which of the brothers he was. After meeting him, I was immediately struck by his unassuming manner and humility. He didn't act at all like a celebrity. As one of the group of freshman we recruited, he attended our smoker that fall but didn't decide to pledge until a year later.

I remember talking with him when he agreed to move from his dorm into the house. Because he was eighteen, I told him we required his parents' signatures on the housing contract. He explained he had become an emancipated minor at age sixteen and informed me he could sign his own contracts. It was the first time I had heard the term and learned its meaning. In addition to being a full-time student, he was still a working musician. Not only did he manage his classes in the School of Music, he played trombone in the IU Marching Hundred band and formed a pickup band that played at Greek dances from time to time. Many weekends he made the nine-hour drive back to Memphis, where he and the MGs were the Stax Records house band. I still marvel at how he successfully he kept all those balls in the air!

Booker T.'s musical talent was exceptional, especially at composition. I recall on several occasions walking through our living room late at night and finding him seated at the grand piano playing a beautiful score. Once, after listening to a few measures of an enchanting melody, I asked him, "What is that you're playing?"

"It's just something I wrote for my composition class," he replied.

"You wrote that?"

T, as we called him then, was also popular with the ladies. I don't know how he carved out the time to have a social life, but he was successful at that too! After I broke up with Gloria, I learned the two of them started seeing each other. Admittedly, I wasn't particularly happy about it, but by then my interest had shifted. I don't remember discussing Gloria with T except for one brief instance. After he had been dating her for a while, he volunteered this comment: "Whew, you really had something!" Nothing further was required.

FIFTY-TWO

SOMETHING COMPLETELY DIFFERENT

WITH TWO MONTHS REMAINING in college, Gloria and I were done, and I was accepted into medical school and passing the second semester of physics. My parents and Mr. Goodman were pleased. Unexpectedly, another freshman girl walked into my life, seemingly out of nowhere. "Nowhere" was actually Greensburg, a small redneck town in southern Indiana that was totally devoid of Blacks. Rumor had it that its last African American resident was lynched in the 1930s. Southern Indiana was a hotbed of Ku Klux Klan activity during the 1920s and 1930s. Entrenched racism had not disappeared thirty years later.

Somehow, this world produced a young woman named Carole Schurch. Her family moved from Louisville, Kentucky, to Greensburg when she was a small child; she had almost no contact with any person of color before she arrived on campus. Once dorm rooms were assigned, she discovered one of her suite mates was "colored," which introduced her to a completely new world that she eagerly embraced. Carole was the first White girl with whom I would develop a romantic relationship. She was cute, about five foot six or five foot seven, with an oval face, short hair, glasses, and a pleasant figure.

From the start there was little subtlety in our relationship. Carole made the first move before I knew who she was. We would usually see each other when we studied in the undergraduate library. After we met, frequent phone conversations followed. Without saying it, her approach suggested she wanted to get together, but I was not convinced if I asked her out she would accept. So I remained hesitant. But by the time the semester was over, we came to know each other quite well. Spending time with Carole gave me confidence that our racial difference would not be a hindrance for us to develop an intimate relationship.

Dating a White or Jewish girl was on the far side of a bridge I had not crossed. At IU, though interracial dating was not common, it did occur. Until I met Carole, I was fearful of three consequences: being turned down, criticism from my Black female friends, and, most importantly, violent pushback from the White community. I came from a setting where an interracial couple was routinely ostracized by both communities. At IU there was no obvious social cost for dating a White girl as long as you remained on campus or at one of the student hangouts nearby. Going deeper into Bloomington was another story. By the end of the school year, Carole had become thoroughly assimilated into Black culture and accepted into our social scene. I don't recall any of my Black female friends objecting to me spending time with her. Carole's wit was caustic.

Our initial attraction was primarily a physical one. Early on she made it clear what kind of a relationship she wanted. We talked frankly about sex. With that goal in mind as the semester was rapidly drawing to a close, we knew there was little time for trivial pleasantries. In the past her assertiveness would have aroused my defenses, but with her it was not the case. She aroused something else! As I came to know her better, I discovered her depth and intellectual acumen to be more profound than I had initially appreciated. Carole was forthright and honest and let me know how she felt. Believing college men were basically corrupt, she considered me exceptional, to the point of being special. We began spending more time together but had yet to have an actual date. I was unsure how or at what speed to proceed, not because of her attitude but because she was White. One day, as we were ending one of our phone conversations, I asked her if she wanted to go out with me. She did.

The plan was to see a movie at a theater just off campus. Ironically, it was *Tom Jones*, a British film about the amorous adventures of a young man. When I called for her on the evening of our first date, I was filled with so much anxious anticipation I could almost taste it. I was about to partake of forbidden fruit. Bouncing into the lounge, she greeted me warmly. My anxiety quickly faded; arm in arm, we were off.

After the movie, as we sat in my car just talking, I sensed an unspoken passion rising between us. This led us to unleash it. Since this was my first date with a White girl, I wondered if it would be any different from my experiences with girls of color. By the end of the evening, I found it was not. I also discovered finding an opportunity to have sex was not the only reason we were attracted to one another. We had become friends. But it was clear having a sexual relationship was high on both our agendas. It would simply require finding a time and place.

We saw each other a lot over the semester's final weeks. Finally, we agreed to take the relationship to the next level. Afterward, it was paramount for me to make sure Carole understood that although the sexual aspect of our relationship was prominent, it was just a part of why I cared for her. She told me she understood. With Carole, I discovered there were gaps in the racial barrier through which both of us could step into a wider world. That would be enough for now.

FIFTY-THREE

IT'S ALL OVER BUT THE SHOUTING

MAY, ONCE AGAIN, WAS upon us. The spring semester was rapidly coming to a close. The final order of official fraternity business was to elect chapter officers for the upcoming year. My year as polemarch was also coming to a close. I took time to revisit and reflect on what had transpired during the year. Recalling the struggles and maneuvering required to cope with the frat's problems, many times I figured the benefits of the office weren't worth the effort I was putting into it. Fortunately, I didn't have to shoulder the effort alone. I came to understand that having individuals you can rely on is key to successfully guiding an organization.

There was an intense competition underway for polemarch. The two candidates were Pat Chavis and Ray Stubbs. Pat's father was an Indianapolis attorney and a prominent Kappa in the national organization. By contrast, Ray, so far as I could determine, was the first White person to become a member of Alpha chapter. He was a southerner from a semirural area of North Carolina. When he indicated an interest in becoming a pledge, saying it was a surprise doesn't do justice to our collective amazement. The ground almost shook!

Accepting him into the Scroller class was more than a little controversial and engendered a lot of heated discussion, both pro and con. I've tried but cannot recall his response when asked the most obvious question: "Why do you want to join a Black fraternity?" Since this was such an unusual occurrence, while writing this memoir I tried to find a way to find the answer. Ray Stubbs and I were never close friends; I have no contact information for him.

After speaking to all those with whom I still have contact who might shed light on the mystery, no one could. Two of my female classmates remembered Ray as pleasant and comfortable around us African Americans, but he never tried to be Black. So far as they could recall, he dated only White girls.

Searching the social media platforms, I located Ray's page on one of them. On it there is a single post where he refers to becoming a Kappa. Just one sentence describes what led to it: "An unanticipated series of events led me to pledge this fraternity." In the end he was accepted as a Scroller and initiated with the rest of his class. Despite this tidbit of information, the mystery remains. Though I recall only fragments of his time in the fraternity, the fact that he became a candidate for polemarch must reflect how well he was received and accepted. Support was evenly split between Ray and Pat. But at the last minute, another candidate entered the race.

John Carter was an active and one of the individuals I had relied on during the previous year. I could always depend on him. Though active in the fraternity, he had little interest in becoming polemarch until Ray became a candidate. Why did John enter the race? It was his fear that Ray might win. John did not want a White guy beating out a Black one for the fraternity presidency and thereby gaining the benefits the leadership position would afford. Realistically, given just the three Black fraternities at IU, the opportunities to reach that office were limited. By comparison, there were almost three dozen White fraternities on campus. Today, John's position might be considered racist bigotry, yet considering the time and place, I understand his rationale.

John was intense and laser focused on his current pursuit, be it academic, political, or social, often to the point of being so matter-of-fact in his manner, he was considered rude. One day prior to the election, he decided to enlist support from the most recently initiated Scrollers to add him as a write-in candidate. He had been the group's pledge dean. He figured their support would provide sufficient votes to win—and it did. He was politically savvy vis-à-vis his election strategy and a keen observer of human behavior. I wasn't surprised when I learned he became an internationally recognized PhD psychologist.

Once the new chapter officers were installed, my overriding emotion was relief. As the final days of my college fraternity life wound to a conclusion, relief gave way to reflection. I took the occasion to consider the fraternity's impact. From the day I became a pledge, it formed the nucleus of my world.

It was the fertile ground where the roots of my college experience took hold. Kappa Alpha Psi accepted me, nurtured me, embraced and supported me. It generated lasting friendships and provided some of my greatest successes. It also created some of my most difficult challenges.

Becoming a Kappa facilitated my entry into student government and confirmed I could function comfortably in a largely White world like the one I would find in medical school. Despite the powerful role Kappa played in my life in college, as that came to an end so did its relevance. The turmoil of the previous years receded into background noise. Going forward, I believed, being a Kappa would have little or no direct role in my immediate future. Consequently, I did not plan to remain an active member.

The last few days wound down, and we prepared to leave. There were no prolonged or emotional farewells with anyone. Most of my friends would return to Bloomington the next fall. Once my exams were completed, I loaded my gear into the car and headed home.

After

FIFTY-FOUR

REFLECTIONS

MY GOALS OF GOING to college and being accepted into medical school were achieved. Still, the most enduring legacy of my years at IU was not my academic success but the social network we students of color fashioned. I can't say my time at IU was representative of the entire Black experience on campus during those years, but it was one thread in the social fabric we fashioned, of which Greek life was an integral part. We did not intend to exclude ourselves from the White college world. More likely from circumstance than design, we became part of a social world apart, connecting with the greater university community when necessary or required.

If there were clues about what the future held for us, we failed to recognize them. We did not know we were unwitting witnesses to the unfolding of the turbulent decade of the 1960s. While we were at IU, the Civil Rights Movement was beginning to gain momentum. The Birmingham children's march occurred on the same weekend as my trip to Central State College in Ohio for May Weekend festivities. Medgar Evers was assassinated in June of 1963 as I was starting my summer job. Though protests against the two years of ROTC still required for most male undergraduates had yet to reach IU, the horror of the Vietnam War was beginning to find its way into America's living rooms on our television screens. We were socially aware, but most of us were not yet activists. As a group and as individuals, some of us quickly learned to manage the social aspect of college, knuckle down, study, and graduate. Some of us didn't.

As it turned out, my years at IU mattered more than I could have imagined. My transition from a naive, wide-eyed freshman to becoming actively involved in campuswide activities and reaching the presidency of my fraternity was not imaginable the day I arrived on campus. Bloomington was the crucible within which the university experience prepared me to move on to medical school. When I reflect on my entire experience at Indiana University, I think of it this way: NBA Hall of Fame basketball player Charles Barkley was asked in an interview if his basketball career was the highlight of his life. Paraphrasing Barkley, I would say of my time at IU, "I may do other things in my life that are more meaningful, but nothing will ever be as much fun."

Before reaching college, I viewed it as a destination, but as I prepared to leave Bloomington, despite its impact and significance, it became clear college was only a stop in the unfolding of my future. I knew the essence of my life was about to undergo a dramatic shift. To start medical school meant I would not return to Bloomington but transition to the medical center in Indianapolis. When I walked into the Medical Science Building on day one, I experienced a rush of emotions over the challenge of becoming a doctor, the most prominent of which were excitement and apprehension. Yet I couldn't help but focus on two things: the impact of my father's driving ambition and the significance of Mr. Goodman's involvement in my life.

If my father's desire was the engine, Mr. Goodman provided the fuel. His presence was like my shadow: always there, sometimes located silently behind me, at other times situated directly in front. When it came to expressing his expectations, he was mostly silent. I recall discussions about the number of credit hours I would take each semester and the costs of housing and supplies, but that's all. I don't remember any discussion of why I planned to become a doctor. His silence suggested it was a given I would pursue a medical career. Without his financial support it's likely none of what I experienced in college would have been possible. I might have been able to complete an undergraduate degree by piecing together student loans, working during the day, and attending classes at night, but it would probably not have involved going to Bloomington or attending medical school.

I never understood the nature of my dad's close relationship with Mr. Goodman. The more I ponder the complexities of their association, the more unanswerable questions I have. Until I began writing this memoir, I accepted

Mr. Goodman's answer to my question about why he chose to help me—that he was doing it as a favor to my father—as the sole motivation for his benevolence. Now, I wonder if there was another more self-centered motive behind his offer. Did he look to me to give him a measure of the satisfaction his children failed to provide? Could there have been yet another reason?

I have discussed his gift with my daughter, who is a licensed psychologist, and she suggested a different motive. Perhaps there was a transactional dynamic between the two men leading to his gift. Was Mr. Goodman in my father's debt for keeping a confidence that he chose to repay through a gift to his son? It would have been a small financial cost to him. My dad impressed me as one who could be trusted to keep a secret. With his vast network of connections, he would know where the bodies were buried. When I considered this more nuanced alternative, the more it seemed plausible that Mr. Goodman's gift was not simply an act of pure altruism from a wealthy Jew to his Black barber. Sadly, anyone who could shed light on this hypothesis has long since passed away, so I'm only left to speculate. I will never know what prompted Mr. Goodman to make his gift. But in the end, I suppose, all that matters is that he did.

EPILOGUE

THE SOCIAL NETWORK THAT had become so important to me was a casualty of moving on to medical school. Like childhood, it could be recalled but not revisited. However, because of it, in concert with the tangible and intangible benefits from my Bloomington years, I was ready to function in this new world. In college I learned to effectively manage my time, to develop my study habits, and to function in an environment free from the more onerous burdens of racism within a society of individuals whose ethnic backgrounds were different from my own.

Once I entered medical school, my world became a lot whiter. There were no instructors of color. In my first-year class of 211 students, there were 3 African Americans, all males. This was the largest number of medical students of color in a single class in the school's history. Only two of us were from IU. It was commonly believed in the Black community that IU's medical school had an unofficial quota for African American students.

During my first semester, the three of us were interviewed by members of a university committee tasked with investigating why the medical school had so few Black applicants. Each of us gave the same answer: "Because you can't get in!" All of us Black students were asked to write a report detailing our views to submit to the committee. A few months later, the official report was released acknowledging the existence of an unofficial quota system for Blacks and pledging to end it with an effort to increase minority enrollment. Despite that commitment, the number of Black medical students had increased only marginally by the time I graduated.

During the next four years, only occasionally did I return to the Bloomington campus, including one trip the following June for commencement to receive my bachelor's degree. My dad must have been one of the proudest fathers in the medical center auditorium on June 10, 1968, when his lifelong dream became a reality, and he witnessed my graduation from medical school. I still see his beaming smile as he stood with Dean Irwin and me for a photo op. Two years earlier, Mr. Goodman had suffered a second heart attack and died. His widow, Mildred, made sure his commitment was fulfilled.

At the start of medical school, our class believed the Vietnam War would be over by the time we finished. Unfortunately, that was 1968. I secured an internship year in Indianapolis, ironically at Methodist Hospital, the same destination of those Sunday afternoon walks with my mother as a little boy, I quickly discovered that without having satisfied a military commitment, upon completing our internships, practically all of us would be drafted into the army. If one hoped to enter a specialty training program after internship, no program chairmen would accept an applicant who hadn't satisfied his military commitment or secured a deferment to complete his training. Realizing that, I enlisted in the US Navy; I would function as a general medical officer, the military equivalent of a primary care physician. After a stint with the Seabees in Vietnam, where the futility of the war effort became clear, I spent the remainder of my two years of active duty at a naval air station in Southern California. Somewhat to my surprise, my navy experience became a postgrad course in how to be a doctor. Upon discharge, I entered a four-year urology residency program at the Medical College of Wisconsin.

Unfortunately, my father did not live to see me complete my specialty training. He passed away in the spring of 1972, during my first year. My mother survived him by twenty-three years; she died at age eighty-five. My residency completed, I moved to Seattle in the summer of 1975 to begin practice. The following year, Lori and I were married.

After thirty-seven years, three children, and two mortgages, I decided it was time to move beyond medicine to explore things I hadn't had the time to pursue. Writing this memoir topped the list. Reliving the emotions and aspirations of my eighteen-, nineteen-, and twenty-year-old self more than fifty years after I recorded them led me to reflect on how time and circumstance had written the story of my life. To have then imagined how the course my life would unfold would have seemed fanciful.

ACKNOWLEDGMENTS

I want to thank these individuals who greatly aided me in filling in the gaps:

Sandra Brown Bender	Gazella Summitt
John Carter	Carole Schurch
Pat Chavis	Charlotte Talley
Sharon Hale Chinn	Ethel Thompson
Ron Finnell	Harold Thompson
Booker T. Jones	Marc Thompson
Lloyd Lyons	Lindsey Thompson
Nancy Lyons	Alvertis "Chickie" Wall
Beverly McKenna	Eileen Baker-Wall
Fay Brownlee Miller	Eleanor Granger-White
Charles O'Bannion	Fletcher Wiley
Joan Stanton Payseur	Aletha Hill Wren

I want to give special thanks to Laurie Burns McRobbie for her enthusiasm for this memoir and her assistance in getting it published.

Finally, I would like to acknowledge my wife, Lori Thompson, for her love and support during this process.

INDEX

Note: Page numbers in *italics* refer to illustrations.

Dr. Lester W. Thompson is a retired Seattle urologist, originally from Indianapolis, Indiana. He received undergraduate and medical degrees from Indiana University in 1965 and 1968. Following two years of active duty in the US Navy, he moved to Seattle and practiced until 2012. Dr. Thompson and his wife, Lori, have three children and four grandchildren.